reconnect

A MARRIAGE COUNSELING WORKBOOK

reconnect

A MARRIAGE COUNSELING WORKBOOK

GUIDED CONVERSATIONS & EXERCISES
for a Long-Lasting Relationship

Zach Brittle, LMHC
&
Laura Heck, LMFT

ZEITGEIST · NEW YORK

This publication contains the opinions and ideas of its authors. It is intended to provide helpful and informative material on the subject matter covered. It is sold with the understanding that the authors and publisher are not engaged in rendering professional services in the book. If the reader requires personal assistance or advice, a competent professional should be consulted. The authors and publisher specifically disclaim any responsibility for any liability, loss, or risk, personal or otherwise, which is incurred as a consequence, directly or indirectly, of the use and application of any of the contents of this book.

Published in the United States by Zeitgeist™, an imprint and division of
Penguin Random House LLC, New York.
zeitgeistpublishing.com

Zeitgeist™ is a trademark of Penguin Random House LLC.
ISBN: 9780593689882

Illustrations © by Liana Nagieva/Shutterstock
Book design by Emma Hall
Author photographs © by Danielle Barnum Photography
Edited by Erin Nelson

Printed in the United States of America
1st Printing

Contents

Introduction

The Key to Connection Is Conversation

THESE DAYS IT'S ALL TOO EASY FOR COUPLES to drift apart and for the daily grind to numb the thrill that once was. But the fact that you're reading this book says something important about you as a couple. You're *committed* to reconnecting and crafting a healthier and more satisfying marriage.

Statistically speaking, couples wait an average of six years before seeking couples therapy. This can be six years of living parallel lives—feeling unseen, lonely, or even experiencing chronic resentment and pain. What keeps couples from getting support? Therapy is hard work because self-reflection and accountability are not for the faint of heart.

This workbook draws on decades of therapeutic practice and research. Zach is a therapist and author who has been teaching and counseling couples for nearly twenty years. Laura is a couples therapist, speaker, curriculum developer, and adventurer in the realm of relationships, sex, and research-based skill and tactics. The two of us have joined forces to coauthor this helpful resource for couples.

We've had thousands of conversations with thousands of people—couples just like you—who have experienced a sense of drifting apart and want to find their way back to one another. What makes this workbook different is that it is for those who probably don't want to sit on a therapy couch but are tired of growing apart.

It's a common hypothesis that poor communication is to blame for drifting apart, but that hasn't been our experience. Plenty of couples "communicate" just fine. They're just using that term to signal the real problem. Where they struggle is "conversation." We've seen couples transform their relationships from distant and disconnected to vibrant and thriving by focusing on one core skill: having meaningful conversation.

The central question that drives this workbook is, "*Why* does meaningful conversation sustain healthy marriages?" Meaningful conversation is the lifeblood of any lasting, loving relationship. It's the space where we lay bare our souls, share our dreams and fears, and truly connect with our partners. Time and time again, we've seen that couples who invest in meaningful conversation find deeper intimacy and profound connection. That's because moving beyond surface-level communication into deeper layers of understanding reveals more of your humanity and desire for connection.

The methods in this workbook are not just empty promises or theoretical concepts. They are rooted in evidence-based exercises and conversations designed to revitalize your marriage. The goal here is clear: build intimacy, trust, and togetherness by sitting down face-to-face and getting to know each other again. You'll rekindle the emotional connection that may have dimmed over the years and, in so doing, reignite the passion that once drew you together.

As you step into the following pages, imagine this workbook as a way to date each other again, bringing intention, wisdom, and curiosity to the forefront—whether you're in the early stages of your relationship or have been married for decades. With each primer exercise and set of conversation questions, you will explore the shared moments that serve as the foundation of your relationship. When you relive your history out loud with each other, you'll take stock of where you have been and where you plan to go—together. Your hearts and minds will find the shared space that has been lost over time. You should feel joy, energy, thrill, and excitement.

The goal of this workbook is to rebuild a shared sense of "This is us." To do that, both of you will be asked two simple questions: Can you allow yourself to be seen and known? Can you enter each conversation with curiosity, love, and kindness? If your answers are not an immediate yes, don't worry. Vulnerability is not created overnight. Each series of conversations will gently encourage vulnerability to grow as you redevelop trust through each exercise.

The by-product of two partners equally exchanging dialogue, curiosity, humor, joy, and exploration is empathy. We'll explore vulnerability and empathy in later chapters, but for now just know you are on your way to being heard and seen and to feeling deeply connected.

Why Do Couples Drift Apart?

It's a fair question, and one we hear a lot. Sometimes couples fall into patterns of conflict or avoidance, where communication becomes a minefield or an empty space. Others might grapple with differences in personality or unique styles of relating, making deeper connection a challenge. Life itself can throw curveballs, overwhelming us with death, illness, or crisis, pushing us further apart when we need each other most. Let's not forget the humdrum nature of daily life, where routines take over and intimacy takes a back seat.

Regardless of a couple's relationship dynamic, one common culprit sits at the center of this gap: a lack of curiosity. As we gather shared experiences as a couple, we often begin to assume that we know just about everything there is to know about each other. Knowing each other's breakfast selection sure can be handy, but that "certainty" you know everything eventually becomes a barrier to deep and vulnerable conversation. When that feeling of certainty is present, we stop seeking new information about our partner and stop demonstrating they are someone worth being known and understood.

Experiencing distance in a relationship can be incredibly disheartening, even painful. It's a reminder of our shared vulnerability. But there's hope. In this journey of reconnection, we won't just tell you to "talk more." Instead, we'll provide you with tools, preparation, and guided conversations. We'll help you build deep and lasting intimacy to make the most of your time.

The Road Back to Each Other

As you flip through the pages of this workbook, take a moment to reflect on how you got here. You likely began your relationship with the highest of hopes; connection seemed to come easily. You were curious about each other, eager to embark on new adventures, and crystal clear about your commitment to a shared future.

Somewhere along the way, something shifted. Everything got harder. The future became hazier. And curiosity took a back seat to the minutiae of the daily grind. We want you to know that no matter who you are or what you've been through, the conversations you will have are a key to rekindling that initial spark and bringing you closer together.

This workbook is for couples who yearn to bridge the gap that has grown between them. It's for those couples who can't seem to talk without arguing or who simply want to disrupt the patterns that have left both parties feeling unheard and unappreciated. It's for those who fear the specter of divorce, the atrophy of intimacy, or the reality of "roommate syndrome." And it's for those who simply want to deepen their alignment and feel the love that brought them together in the first place. No matter where you fall within these categories, the power of meaningful conversation is within your grasp.

How to Use This Book

Think of part 1 as the preparatory phase before embarking on a cross-country road trip. You wouldn't set out without ensuring your oil had been changed and your tires were properly balanced. And unless you've had lots of practice, you'll pack and repack several times just to make sure you have enough socks and underwear.

In the same way, these first two short chapters prepare you for the journey ahead, offering you the tools and insights you need to get the most out of your conversations. The foundation you build in part 1 is essential for smooth sailing through the rest of the book.

Imagine part 2 as a well-curated itinerary for your trip, one that takes you on a journey through the trajectory of your relationship. This part consists of five chapters, each corresponding to a different stage in your love story. Within these chapters, you'll find dozens of relationship-building conversations that provide structure, guidance, and inspiration. Each conversation is structured as follows:

* **A Topic:** This is the central theme that the conversation will revolve around. It can range from discussing your dreams to addressing past conflicts.
* **A Primer Exercise:** This exercise will foster togetherness and provide a supportive framework for the conversation. It's like stretching before a workout, ensuring your emotional muscles are limber and ready to engage. If the activity requires writing, pass the workbook between you.
* **Conversation Questions:** These questions are your road map for the conversation. They are carefully crafted to spark meaningful dialogue and encourage a deeper understanding of each other. Take turns asking each other a question aloud (e.g., "How do you feel when I show you affection?") and take turns answering from your own perspectives. When prompted, brainstorm your answers as a couple (e.g., "What would we consider a major turning point in our relationship?"). Be sure to give each other enough floor space to fully share your thoughts and ideas and ask relevant questions. Carry on the conversation from there. Take it one question at a time and return to any that one or both of you might need to process first. It isn't necessary to address *every* question in a section in one sitting.

* **A Ritual of Connection:** This is a special personal ritual that aligns with the topic. These rituals add depth and meaning to your conversations.

While part 2 chronologically reflects the stages of a relationship, you can choose your own adventure to best suit your current needs and circumstances. The important thing is to actively engage in meaningful conversations. Remember, this journey is uniquely yours, and these conversations will help you rediscover the love that initially brought you together.

Feel free to dive right into part 2 if you're eager to get talking. However, we encourage you to review the Pre-Conversation Checklist on page 50 first. It's like checking that you have a full tank of emotional fuel before embarking on the journey.

Committing to This Process with You

Take a moment to reflect on your intention for yourself as you use this workbook. We want you to come closer together and find safety and meaning throughout this process, and one way to do that is to identify how you want to show up for each other.

When you set an intention for yourself, you have someone to be accountable to: YOU. So take a moment to be mindful of your own thoughts, feelings, and actions. The following series of statements will help you narrow your focus and declare your aspirations for the relationship as you learn the skill of conversation.

1. I understand that this workbook will lead me through conversations with my partner, intended to deepen our connection and intimacy. My intention for myself throughout this process is:

Partner A	**Partner B**
______________________	______________________
______________________	______________________
______________________	______________________
______________________	______________________
______________________	______________________
______________________	______________________

2. The best version of me that needs to show up in this process can be described as (e.g., kind, gentle, nonjudgmental, open):

Partner A	Partner B
______	______
______	______
______	______
______	______

3. I am aware of barriers (e.g., time, patience, lack of vulnerability, past pain, or resentment) that may get in the way of my intention, and I plan to remove these barriers in this way:

Partner A	Partner B
______	______
______	______
______	______

4. This is how I want our relationship to look after completing this workbook:

Partner A	Partner B
______	______
______	______
______	______

Part 1

HOW TO HAVE SUCCESSFUL CONVERSATIONS

This part lays the critical foundation for deep and meaningful connections. It emphasizes the core elements of human connection:

* **Curiosity:** Genuine interest in your partner's thoughts and feelings keeps conversations alive. It shows a keen desire to understand each other.
* **Accountability:** Taking responsibility for your actions and acknowledging your role in the relationship is key to resolving conflicts and building trust through open and honest communication.
* **Vulnerability:** To have truly meaningful conversations, you must be willing to be vulnerable, sharing your innermost thoughts and feelings, which allows your partner to see your authentic self.

The tools provided in this part are universal and apply to all couples, whether you're in the early stages of your relationship or celebrating a milestone anniversary next month.

Foundational principles remain constant, and while part 1 isn't a comprehensive discussion of therapeutic themes and strategies, it equips you with the essentials to make immediate improvements in your marriage. These principles—curiosity, accountability, and vulnerability—are the keys to unlocking deeper and more meaningful conversations, offering a path to a stronger and more connected relationship.

CHAPTER 1

The Three Principles of Healthy Connection

This chapter unveils the core principles that lead to deeply satisfying conversations. These principles lay the groundwork for forging bonds that are rich in trust, understanding, and love. When we embark on the journey of rebuilding connection, it's crucial to redefine what we mean by "successful" conversations. In this chapter, we'll peel back the layers of this term and then set the stage for what to strive for in your conversations.

A Closer Look at "Success"

Many couples avoid conversation because, if it doesn't go well, they think it's a failure. But when attempting to reconnect, there is no failure; there are only steps in the learning process. Think of it as a skill like any other that you need to practice. Even if a conversation doesn't go as planned, it can still be an opportunity for growth and understanding.

When pursuing deeper connection, it's important to remember that it's normal for conflicts to arise along the way. Conflict is not a sign of failure; in many instances, it can be a sign of growth. When handled constructively, conflict can lead to greater intimacy. In fact, sometimes it's necessary to address underlying issues to clear the path for deeper connection.

So what should couples strive for in their conversations? Here, success is not about winning arguments or always seeing eye to eye. Instead, it's about fostering joy, curiosity, empathy, and, ultimately, a deep sense of togetherness and feeling understood. It's about nurturing your emotional connection, creating moments of vulnerability and trust, and learning something new about yourself, your partner, and your relationship.

As you dive deeper into this workbook, remember that the goal isn't necessarily to avoid conflict, and it isn't about achieving perfection. It's about creating moments that truly matter and that bring you closer together in love and understanding.

Principle 1: Remain Curious

In our quest for more meaningful conversations and deeper connection within our marriages, one of the most vital principles is curiosity. Not only does curiosity spark the initial attraction in a relationship, but it is also instrumental in maintaining and enriching it over time. Here curiosity is about more than just being good at asking questions. It's the desire to understand and explore your partner's world, thoughts, and feelings.

It's about staying open to the possibility that there is always something to learn about each other.

Some clients start couples therapy being *sure* of what their partner is going to do or say. They have supreme confidence that they already know all their partners' stories. Their conviction that they know their partner so well means that they stop asking questions and rest comfortably in their assumptions. This is what we call the "sin of certainty," and it kills intimacy.

When you are curious about your partner, however, you suspend certainty long enough to create a safe space for them to explore and expose their deeper layers. Being curious encourages open dialogue as you ask questions and listen actively. In this way, curiosity isn't about satisfying your own interests or preconceptions; rather, it's about exploring and cherishing your partner's interests, experiences, and emotions.

What's more, curious couples tend to be happier, and here's why: when you notice the small things about your partner's world, such as their likes and dislikes, their closest friends, or their work-related stressors, you're sending a powerful message: "You matter, and I care about you." This form of attentiveness builds trust, intimacy, and a deep sense of togetherness. It demonstrates that you are not just present but genuinely invested in each other's happiness and well-being. This kind of communication fosters genuine interest in your partner and forms the bedrock of a strong and lasting relationship.

So as you navigate your relationship, consider the role of curiosity, keeping in mind that it can manifest in small, everyday acts as well as in grand gestures. When you embrace the small and big moments of understanding, you'll find that the power of curiosity can breathe new life into your connection, one conversation at a time.

Deepening Love through Curiosity

In every marriage, the interplay of love and like creates a dynamic and reinforcing cycle. While love forms the bedrock of your connection, liking your partner—enjoying their company and nurturing fondness for them—is what keeps the flame of your relationship alive. Curiosity deepens this affection and contributes to a more satisfying and enduring marriage. To inspire fondness between each other and deepen your love, consider these approaches:

- **Practice generosity:** When it's your turn to talk, be generous with your thoughts, experiences, and feelings. Give your partner the opportunity to practice curiosity. When it's your turn to listen, be generous with your attention. Show your partner that you care about their thoughts and feelings and give them the gift of validation.

- **Surprise each other:** Start with small surprises or thoughtful gestures that cater to your partner's interests or preferences. These unexpected acts of kindness create a habit of discovery that bleeds into the overall relationship.

- **Schedule time for curiosity and take turns:** Nearly everyone schedules things that are important to them (e.g., workouts, meals, coffee with friends). Make sure to also schedule uninterrupted time to practice curiosity and be sure to keep track of whose turn it is to speak and whose turn it is to listen.

- **Prioritize gratitude:** When you nurture gratitude for what you have, it softens the focus on what you don't have. You'll see what you're looking for, so go ahead and look for the qualities you admire in your partner. And then say, "Thank you."

As you embrace curiosity and actively engage with these practices, you'll find that loving *and* liking each other become intertwined, reinforcing love and like in a harmonious cycle. Your marriage will become a space of profound connection, enduring love, and genuine fondness, making your journey together more fulfilling.

Over the course of your relationship, recall one specific event when you were proud to be with your partner. Briefly describe this event inside the circle. In each of the three rectangles, identify one of your partner's characteristics that you adore most and that showed up during this event. Explain to your partner in as much detail as possible why these characteristics are so meaningful to you. The details around why you adore, admire, respect, and cherish these qualities are a surefire way to deepen your bond. Here's an example:

MY BROTHER'S WEDDING IN 2019

Charismatic

Spontaneous

Sexy

Why I adore, admire, respect, and cherish these qualities (spoken aloud):

I love to meet new people with you because you are so charismatic and connect so quickly and easily with others that it puts me at ease. I appreciate your playful spontaneity because it forces me out of my comfort zone. I am very attracted to you physically when I see how confident you are in your body, especially when I dance with you.

Why I adore, admire, respect, and cherish these qualities (spoken aloud):

PARTNER A

Why I adore, admire, respect, and cherish these qualities (spoken aloud):

PARTNER B

Replacing Judgment with Curiosity

The goal of conflict is not to convince your partner that you are right or even to solve a problem. The goal of conflict is to remain connected while also getting your needs met. This often involves compromise, and curiosity is the golden ticket here. If curiosity is *not* present, even well-meaning, loving couples can slip into judgment or righteousness, which can invalidate and dismiss their partner's unique experience.

Be on the lookout for judgment in conversation, as it can be quite sneaky! Here's an example:

> **Statement:** "My boss just moved all one-on-one meetings to 8:00 a.m., and now I can't go for my morning runs."
>
> **Judgmental response:** "It's heading into winter anyway; you won't want to wake up to run in the cold."

This person's response dismisses how important morning runs are to their partner.

> **Curious response:** "I know how much you enjoy your morning runs. How do you feel about that?"

This response opens the door for exploration and conversation that helps your partner to feel known. Asking "How does that make you feel?" helps you stay curious about your partner's experience while suspending your assumptions.

When you lead with curiosity, it sends the message that your partner is someone worth knowing. There are few things more powerful in this world.

Noticing You, Loving You

Here's a series of fun questions for you and your partner to explore how well you know each other. Ask these questions of each other aloud. Jot your answers down on separate pieces of paper. Afterward, share your responses question by question. Remember that your answers may be inaccurate! That's okay. This is an opportunity to be curious and say, "Tell me more about that."

1. Am I a night owl or early bird?
2. Do you prefer to cook or would you rather I cook?
3. What is my favorite holiday?
4. What is my favorite gift I ever received?
5. What was my favorite book growing up?
6. How do I feel about getting older?
7. How do I feel about my relationship with my parents?
8. Where am I eager to go on vacation?
9. Which educator had the most impact on my life?
10. What is the most trouble I got into as a child?
11. What current world events do I find most troubling?
12. How do I self-soothe when feeling overwhelmed or stressed out?

Principle 2: Hold Yourself Accountable

Point your finger at the wall and look at your hand. Likely, one finger is pointing away from you, and three more are pointing back at you. This is how to be successful in a relationship. Relationships thrive when each partner is more focused on taking personal accountability for their own feelings and behaviors than on finger-pointing and demanding change.

We often have couples who come into our offices in a stalemate, saying, "I'm not willing to put any more effort into this relationship until my partner does *X*." That's when we know it's time for a paradigm shift toward introspection. The greatest avenue for change in your relationship starts and ends with your ability to look inward and focus on what you have control over.

Why are finger-pointing and blame so much easier than looking inward and taking accountability? Accepting fault in ourselves requires a strong sense of self-worth that recognizes that we did something wrong, not that we are inherently bad. Human beings will do just about anything to avoid the shame that accompanies the internalized limiting beliefs of "I'm unworthy," "I'm a screwup," "I'm not enough," and "I'm too much to handle." This is why finger-pointing at our partner is so much easier. It allows us to deflect the familiar feelings of shame that get stirred up in conflict.

Here is an example of what personal accountability looks like in a tense conversation between Robin and Jesse. Notice that neither partner is blaming the other. Instead, they are each sharing their own thoughts, feelings, and perceptions.

ROBIN: "I acknowledge that I raised my voice and called you names. I realize now that I was hurt by you walking away from me and not responding to my questions. I told myself the story that I was in trouble for something that I did."

JESSE: "I did walk away from you and was purposefully not responding. I know that it hurts you when I do that. To be honest, I was so overwhelmed I didn't want to respond and make things worse."

Robin and Jesse's example beautifully illustrates Robin's self-awareness of the story "I'm in trouble," and Robin shares this with Jesse. Jesse has self-awareness of being emotionally incapable of communicating effectively and made a choice to shut down and withdraw from the conversation.

If you struggle with shameful feelings and find personal accountability difficult, start with self-compassion. The same way we're asking you to meet each other with curiosity, we want you each to meet your own feelings and thoughts with curiosity instead of judgment. Be gentle with yourself. Robin's self-compassion makes it possible to acknowledge that raising one's voice and name-calling are behaviors, not a characterization of who Robin is as a person. Robin's curiosity then allows further exploration of why Jesse's withdrawal caused such a strong reaction. Robin's self-gentleness also helps Robin accept that hurt is a valid emotion in response to an unresponsive partner *and* that it is *not* okay within the contract of their marriage to name-call.

Accountability is primarily about making sure you focus more on the part *you* play in any given conflict or situation than on the part played by the other person. In this way, you lay the groundwork for building trust and reinforcing commitment in the relationship.

Create a Safe Space to Share

Practicing vulnerability can be hard work. One way to make it more manageable is to create an emotional environment that is welcoming for both of you. Here are several ways to encourage emotional safety for each other:

Turn toward each other: The term "turn toward" comes from the work of Drs. John and Julie Gottman. The Gottmans are the gold standard in the field of relationship research, and we'll reference them often throughout this workbook. "Turning toward" quite literally means turning your body toward your partner and giving them your attention. It also means that whenever your partner asks for attention (we call those *bids*), you respond by providing evidence that you are paying attention and that their needs matter to you. In this way you're closing the loop of connection and building trust. These simple acts of turning toward and responding as often as possible to your partner's bids is the foundation of building trust that, when you emotionally reach for your partner, they will be there.

Anytime your partner makes an emotional bid, big or small, respond immediately, even if the response is a rain check—e.g., "I would love to go for a walk with you. I'm in the middle of a lengthy work email, so would you mind if we go in an hour?"

Consider your body language: Humans have a highly sensitive nervous system, which includes the brain, spinal cord, and a complex network of messengers and receptors that are silently running in the background and affecting our subconscious reactions. Our nervous system is responsible for scanning the environment for threats so that we can respond quickly enough to stay safe. Body language tells our nervous system a lot about another's intentions toward us. In this way, your body language can either calm your partner's nervous system or send signals of danger.

Common threatening body language includes standing and puffing up, pacing, large or sweeping arm motions, lack of eye contact, hand-wringing, or hiding hands (e.g., hands in pockets or tucked under your crossed arms). On the other hand, calm can be communicated by maintaining a gentle tone, breathing slowly, opening your palms, and physically turning your face and body toward the other person.

Have a conversation about what type of body language each of you perceives as calming and threatening.

Practice nondefensive listening: Nondefensive listening is a shift from listening to find fault, playing devil's advocate, or poking holes in your partner's logic to listening to find something you agree with or can react to by saying, "That's a good point." Help your partner feel safe opening up and sharing even controversial topics with you by taking an agreeable stance. If you find yourself getting defensive, it may mean you don't have enough information. Try saying, "I'm listening. Share more." And then bite your tongue and bring all your attention to your ears.

Initiate a repair: Think of repair as literally repairing a rift in the relationship. This may be as simple as agreeing to slow down, reminding each other that you can get through this, or even deciding to take an extended break. No matter how or why you've drifted away from each other, repair is the act of mutually coming back together—of repairing without focusing on resolving. You don't have to be expert communicators to create emotional safety; you just have to be committed to pausing long enough to assure each other that you're essentially decent people who can be trusted to behave thoughtfully and kindly when you mess up. Agree that when one or both of you veer off into dangerous territory, both of you are going to make consistent attempts to make it better. Practice taking accountability for your errors by saying, "I screwed that up . . . let me try that again."

Offer validation: Validating your partner means saying yes to them in some way, shape, or form. This doesn't have to be "yes" as much as it needs to be some acknowledgment that they are bringing value to the conversation. This is perhaps one of the hardest lessons for couples to master. You don't get to argue or talk your partner out of their feelings. What you can do is create emotional safety for each other by accepting your partner's feelings exactly as they are. This means not minimizing, dismissing, or trying to talk your partner out of their feelings. Consider this example:

> ROBIN SAYS: "I really miss our evening walks when we could just talk without interruption."
>
> JESSE'S DISMISSIVE RESPONSE: "Oh, it's not that bad. The kids are getting more self-sufficient and interrupt us less and less these days."
>
> JESSE'S VALIDATING RESPONSE: "Me too. It's a challenge with the kids around, but I bet we can figure out how to have uninterrupted time if we brainstorm a bit."

Here's an important tip: Try to focus on the *emotion* rather than the logistics (e.g., "I can see how you would miss our walks; we used to have such great chats").

Before you move on, take a quick personal inventory. On a scale of 1 (low) to 5 (high), rate how you think you are currently doing in each principle of creating emotional safety:

	PARTNER A	PARTNER B
Turn toward		
Body language		
Non-defensive listening		
Repair		
Validation		

The Tenets of Respectful Communication

Review these eight tenets of respectful communication together. Brainstorm two more that are important to each of you as a couple on this journey and write them down in the spaces provided. Sign on the dotted line to show each other that you agree to honor these tenets of respectful communication throughout this workbook and beyond in your marriage. To reinforce this agreement, take a photo of this page, print it out, and hang it somewhere highly visible as a reminder of your promise to each other.

1. I commit to speaking from the "I" position. I will talk about *my* thoughts and feelings and refrain from any theories or assumptions or statements about "you."
2. I will allow you to finish what you want to say without interrupting.
3. I will avoid inflammatory language (e.g., name-calling, cursing, or saying, "You always . . ." "You never . . ." or "You should . . . ")
4. I will always find a way to agree with some small part of what you are saying (e.g., "*X* makes sense" or "I can see what you mean by *X*").
5. I will choose empathy over problem-solving and try to identify with what you are feeling before attempting to help fix your issues.
6. I will pause before responding to avoid defensiveness or misinterpretation. I will reflect what I hear to ensure the opportunity for repair in the event the impact was different from the intent.
7. I will share my feelings about the situation, rather than my interpretations of what's going on, and will commit to being clear about my own feelings and experiences without escalating. This will allow you to understand me better and respond with compassion and empathy.
8. I will listen to understand and not to respond. I will delay the impulse to justify, argue, defend, or explain my point of view to fully make room for yours.
9. ______________________________

   ____
10. ______________________________

   ____

SIGNED: ______________________ DATED: __________

SIGNED: ______________________ DATED: __________

Understand Your Limits

Let's take a moment to dig a bit deeper into the autonomic nervous system (ANS) and the importance of recognizing its impact on your ability to be respectful during a conversation. For starters, here's a comparison of respectful communication with communication that has become dysregulated because the ANS has detected a threat:

RESPECTFUL COMMUNICATION	DYSREGULATED COMMUNICATION
Empathetic	Focused only on your own point of view
Reasonable	Superlatives and cursing
Validating	Repeating yourself
Calm voice	Raised voice
Focused on partner	Can't hear as well
Quick to repair	Can't think clearly
Open to compromise	Escalated physiology (e.g., crossing arms)

The function of the ANS is to regulate unconscious tasks like breathing and heart rate. It also initiates the fight-or-flight response when it perceives a threat (real or imagined) by stimulating the sympathetic nervous system. This activates a series of powerful physiological responses that prepare us to survive, including the secretion of the hormones epinephrine (aka adrenaline) and cortisol. Among other effects, this causes an increase in heart rate.

At this point, stress is soaring high. It's almost as if your body and brain have been hijacked by your sympathetic nervous system. The collateral damage of this physiological reaction is a lack of curiosity, empathy, humor, and logic. In the face of perceived danger, your brain has the solo task of keeping you safe and no longer has the capacity to communicate respectfully.

The goal is to develop self-awareness when you become activated and slip into this heightened survival state. The signs of the fight-or-flight response are varied. They may be bodily sensations (e.g., tight jaw, sweating, feeling flushed), emotional disorientation (e.g., repeating yourself, feeling confused, loss of short-term memory), or any sense of feeling unsafe.

Common fight-or-flight responses include:

FIGHT RESPONSES	FLIGHT RESPONSES
Accusations	Avoidance of eye contact
Aggressive body language	Becoming overly busy or preoccupied
Bringing up past mistakes	Developing passive-aggressive behavior
Contemptuous expressions	Emotional numbing
Criticism and blame	Engaging in risky behaviors
Defensive behavior	Engaging in self-harm
Emotional manipulation	Escaping through work or hobbies
Intense arguing	Ignoring messages or calls
Name-calling	Leaving the room or space
Physical aggression	Physically distancing oneself
Raised voice or yelling	Seeking emotional support from others
Refusal to compromise	Shutting down
Retaliation	Silent treatment
Stonewalling	Substance use or abuse
Verbal confrontation	Withdrawing emotionally

Using different-colored pens and taking turns, circle any of the responses that feel familiar to you. Compare your responses. Discuss anything new you learned about yourself or your partner.

The biggest struggle couples encounter is *not* that they get activated and slip into fight-or-flight mode; it's that they remain activated and continue to try to communicate. Remember your agreement to uphold the tenets of respectful communication. This contract is impossible to keep if you're activated. Therefore, you need to agree to take space from each other to calm your nervous system. Then, once you are regulated, you can come back together.

Most humans can regulate their nervous system within 20 minutes of conscious self-soothing. When you're physiologically aroused, the first step is getting your body back so that you can think clearly about your next steps. What can you do for 20 minutes that would be truly relaxing and soothing? Some ideas include deep breathing, meditating, walking, scrolling through social media, praying, doing yoga, petting the dog or cat, and reading.

You may be concerned that we just gave one or both of you an excuse to exit the conversation, which is a bad habit that plagues many relationships. However, this doesn't mean that one partner can opt out of a relational moment without the other partner's consent and a promise to return to the discussion. In fact, exercising a purposeful "pause for cooling down" is the epitome of respectful communication, because it respectfully communicates that you are activated and need to calm down.

Learn When to Pause

Respectfully declaring a pause for cooling down is simple: Clearly communicate to your partner the facts (e.g., "I am feeling overwhelmed"), request a pause (e.g., "I need a break to calm down"), and promise to return (e.g., "Let's come back in 20 minutes").

Work together to co-construct a few ways to communicate to each other when you are feeling hijacked by your nervous system and you need a break to reregulate. The agreement here is that you will prioritize the pause in communication to allow your body to cool down before reengaging in respectful communication.

1. ______________________________

2. ______________________________

3. ______________________________

We agree to prioritize respectful communication by recognizing when we are in fight-or-flight mode, to make one of the above requests, and then to pause for 20 minutes to calm down before reengaging each other in the discussion.

SIGNED: ______________________ DATED: __________

SIGNED: ______________________ DATED: __________

Principle 3: Practice Vulnerability

Vulnerability might seem lofty or unattainable, but it's really just a skill—and like any other skill, it requires practice. It's about being open, honest, and emotionally transparent with your partner. While it may sound daunting, being vulnerable isn't something you are or aren't. Vulnerability exists on a spectrum, and our ability to practice it waxes and wanes. The ability to be vulnerable depends on a variety of factors, such as how safe we feel, our current mental and physical state, and the quality of our relationship.

Vulnerability is *not* about sharing your deepest fears and insecurities every moment of the day. Rather, it's about creating a space whereby both partners can be genuine and open to:

- **Sharing feelings:** Expressing emotions honestly, even if they are scary.
- **Asking for help:** Allowing your partner to support you in both practical and personal ways.
- **Seeking repair:** Attempting to come back together with your partner in a healthy way and allowing that attempt to be successful.

Practicing vulnerability in marriage offers numerous benefits. It strengthens the emotional connection between you and your partner, fostering intimacy and trust. It allows you to see and accept each other as you truly are, reducing the need for pretenses or defenses. This kind of emotional honesty can lead to more profound understanding and empathy in your relationship.

Practicing vulnerability in a marriage can have a ripple effect in your family legacy. As you and your partner become more comfortable with being open and honest with each other, this newfound intimacy can positively influence other aspects of your life. You'll likely find that you can more readily share your thoughts and feelings with friends and family, and you'll be better equipped to navigate challenging situations both inside and outside your marriage.

Why Is It So Hard to Be Vulnerable?

Let's not mince words—practicing vulnerability is hard for anyone, and even more so within a marriage. This difficulty is normal and arises from experiences we collect through the years. For example, your early experiences as a child might have made you feel uncomfortable expressing your emotions. If you weren't encouraged to honestly share your feelings as a kid or had to sacrifice your own feelings to stay physically or emotionally safe, it's no wonder you struggle to be vulnerable as an adult. Vulnerability can feel like a foreign language, making it even more uncomfortable to convey who we are, how we feel, and what we need.

Past trauma can play a big role in how comfortable you are exposing your true self to another person. Varying degrees of violation, betrayal, or heartache can make someone cautious about opening up in relationships. The fear of being hurt or taken advantage of again can lead to a natural hesitancy to practice vulnerability. In the battle of safety over vulnerability, safety almost always wins.

We live in a world that places great emphasis on being "strong" and self-reliant. This can lead to the belief that vulnerability is a sign of weakness. Many people fear judgment and rejection from our partners and society if we expose our sensitivities and true selves. These factors reinforce how important it is to remember that vulnerability is a skill that can develop over time. Remember that it's okay to take small steps toward vulnerability and that your partner may be experiencing similar challenges.

Vulnerability Is Learned

It's natural to wonder if it's possible to become more vulnerable in your relationship, especially if you've been guarding your emotions for some time. The good news is that vulnerability can be developed and refined over time. Here are a few ways to begin practicing vulnerability and witnessing its positive effects:

* **Start small.** You don't have to dive headfirst into deep, personal revelations. Begin with the stuff that feels easier and grow from there with practice.
* **Practice listening.** Vulnerability isn't just about sharing; it's also about receiving. When you create a safe space for each other, you each gain access to more profound aspects of yourselves.
* **Express gratitude.** Make it a habit to express gratitude for each other's presence in your life. This simple act fosters a sense of emotional connection and primes the environment for vulnerability.
* **Ask for help.** You've already taken a step in the right direction by doing the exercises in this workbook, but, if needed, don't be afraid to involve a trained couples therapist who can guide you in practicing vulnerability and improving communication in your marriage.

By taking small steps and gradually increasing your level of openness, you can experience the transformative power of vulnerability within your marriage and beyond.

Levels of Connection

Emotional intimacy is the heart and soul of any deeply connected relationship. Without it, physical and sexual intimacy can often lack the depth and richness that makes it truly fulfilling. This is where practicing vulnerability plays a crucial role, not only in building emotional intimacy but also in enhancing physical connection. Here are a few things to keep in mind as you move forward:

* **Vulnerability builds trust and safety.** When you trust each other emotionally, you are more likely to trust each other sexually as well. This trust can translate into a deeper physical and sexual connection, as you can be fully present and open.

- **Vulnerability builds deeper understanding.** When you risk going deeper with your feelings and become clearer about your desires, needs, and boundaries, you actually create more space for safety and security, which is a core element of physical and sexual intimacy.
- **Vulnerability improves communication.** As you each share your vulnerabilities, you gain access to an expanded emotional vocabulary, which can lead to improved communication and empathy and ultimately a more satisfying physical relationship.

In part 2, the conversations are designed to foster emotional intimacy and trust, making vulnerability a key element. By engaging in these conversations, you can not only strengthen your emotional connection but also set the stage for more fulfilling physical interactions. Our goal for you is that this approach to connection will lead to a thriving relationship in all areas of your life.

The Vulnerability Scale

Take turns reading and responding to the following statements to see where each of you falls on the vulnerability scale. There are no right or wrong answers here, only information about where there is room for growth.

1. When faced with a challenge:
   a) I open up and share my concerns and feelings with my partner.
   b) I share some aspects of the challenge but keep certain feelings to myself.
   c) I prefer to handle challenges independently before sharing them with my partner.

2. I find it easy to express my emotions, even if they make me feel vulnerable:
   a) Always
   b) Sometimes
   c) Rarely

3. When my partner is upset or needs emotional support:
   a) I listen actively, empathize, and offer my support.
   b) I listen and offer support, but I may not fully understand their feelings.
   c) I struggle to provide emotional support and may avoid the conversation.

4. Sharing my deepest fears or insecurities with my partner:
   a) Feels natural and strengthens our connection.
   b) Feels uncomfortable, but I've done it on occasion.
   c) Is something I've rarely, if ever, done.

5. I initiate conversation with my partner about my feelings or concerns:
   a) Frequently. I prioritize open communication in our relationship.
   b) Occasionally. I'm comfortable discussing some topics but not others.
   c) Rarely. I tend to avoid discussing personal matters with my partner.

6. In our relationship, I typically handle conflict:
   a) By engaging in open and respectful dialogue to resolve issues.
   b) By avoiding conflict or withdrawing to avoid escalation.
   c) By becoming defensive or confrontational during disagreements.

7. Expressing affection and appreciation toward my partner:
   a) Feels very comfortable. I regularly express my love and gratitude.
   b) Feels somewhat comfortable, but I may hold back on expressing affection at times.
   c) Feels uncomfortable; I struggle to convey my feelings openly.

Scoring

Mostly A: You are in the "open and vulnerable" category. You are comfortable sharing your thoughts and feelings with your partner, and vulnerability is an integral part of your relationship.

Mostly B: You are in the "moderately vulnerable" category. You are open to vulnerability but may have some reservations or find it challenging at times.

Mostly C: You are in the "less vulnerable" category. You may struggle with being open and vulnerable in your relationship.

Remember that vulnerability is a skill that can be developed with practice. As you progress through this workbook and continue to engage in meaningful conversations, you may find your relationship to vulnerability evolving. Revisit this quiz after completing the workbook to track your growth and increased openness.

CHAPTER 2

Preparing for Connection

Before engaging in the exercises and conversations in part 2, let's delve into the importance of preparing your physical and emotional space. Just as packing the essentials for your trip helps ensure that you get the most out of your journey, setting the context for heartfelt conversation and meaningful connection is essential to reaping the full benefits of this journey.

By taking manageable proactive steps, you and your partner can create an environment where trust, empathy, and understanding will flourish. This chapter guides you through practical strategies to create this space, ensuring that your interactions are open, authentic, and productive.

A Comfortable, Enjoyable Environment

Creating a comfortable and enjoyable physical and emotional space for meaningful conversations is essential. It's like setting the table for a special meal. You'd want everything to reflect the tone of the occasion, and you'd remove any potential distractions. Keeping this in mind, here are some questions to consider as you shape your ideal space:

1. Where can we go that is quiet and private for our meaningful conversations and to do these exercises together?
2. What physical elements will enhance our space (e.g., comfortable seating, soft lighting)?
3. Are there any potential sources of discomfort or tension in these surroundings that we need to address/remedy (e.g., removing clutter or distractions)?

Jot down your notes on your ideal space here:

Our space to have meaningful conversations is ______________________

____

To ensure privacy, we will ______________________________

____

To enhance our space, we'll include __________________________

____

We'll address any discomfort or distractions by ____________________

____

Remember, these conversations aren't just an exercise; they're an opportunity to deepen your connection, strengthen your relationship, and rediscover the joy of being with each other. Set the stage in a way that gets you excited about the prospect of diving into this journey together. You're about to embark on a path that will bring you closer, helping you rediscover the joy, curiosity, and love that first brought you together.

Rituals of Connection

The Gottmans' research reveals a way to quantify emotional connection between partners. Imagine that your relationship has a shared bank account, the emotional bank account. All the positive moments of affection, humor, love, and appreciation serve as deposits. All the disrespectful communication, emotional distancing, and bad behavior are withdrawals from the bank account. Ideally, your emotional bank account always has a positive balance, so that when you have a crummy day and you are extra sensitive, the emotional withdrawals don't overdraw your bank account, leaving you with a deficit.

This theory comes down to working smarter, not harder, through a series of habitual "auto deposits." In *The Power of Habit*, Charles Duhigg outlines how to make long-term, major life changes by activating small, powerful habits done consistently. Habit creation is conscious at first, but over time it requires less and less effort to engage and drifts into the flow of everyday life.

The auto deposits in your relationship are small, habitual moments of deep connection that occur regardless of life's disruption and chaos. For example, one couple has a habit of walking every evening after dinner, rain or shine (mostly because the dogs need a walk), but it serves as a solid time to chat about the day. Another couple has a habit of celebrating their wedding anniversary by watching the same movie and dining at the fanciest restaurant they could afford twenty-five years earlier. These auto deposits, coupled with others throughout the course of an ordinary day, week, month, or year, help these couples maintain a surplus of deposits in their emotional bank accounts.

What two established habits do you have as a couple as a means of deep connection that help you fund your emotional bank account?

1. ______________________________

2. ______________________________

Brainstorm five new habits that will help you create a deeper connection:

1. ______________________________

2. ______________________________

3. ______________________________

4. ______________________________

5. ______________________________

Our Time Together

It's time to get specific about how you would like to engage with this workbook as a couple. Aligning your vision of how you would like to move through these exercises and conversations together reduces the risk of unmet expectations. Here are a few suggestions for success:

- **Commit to a consistent day and time.** What time of day works best for both of you to avoid distractions and fatigue? Which days are the most open? Choose a day and time, and prioritize this time together the same way you would prioritize an appointment with your accountant or doctor. Put it on the calendar, clear away distractions, and come prepared.

Small Things, Often

Laura conducted an informal survey of married partners for a project called the "Epic Wives Experiment" a few years back. One of her favorite questions was, "How do you know you are loved?" She was shocked by the simple responses: "Makes me coffee in the morning," "Scratches my back at night," "Asks me if I need anything at the store," "Asks me how my day was," "Holds my hand in the car," "Invites me to take a walk," "Initiates sex," and so on.

The purpose of this inquiry was to help convince the participants in the experiment that the way love was received was not about occasional grandiose gestures but about consistent small gestures. At the heart of these small gestures was the message "You matter to me."

To help you better understand the impact of small gestures of love, take turns answering these questions and discuss your individual responses:

- What is something I can do to show you love in the morning?
- When we are apart all day, how can I remind you that I care about you?
- How can I express my affection without sexual touching?
- What makes you feel most connected to me in the evenings and on weekends?
- What has historically been your favorite way to receive love from me?

* **Activate the best version of you.** Are you calm, relaxed, and focused? If not, what might you need to do to show up as the best version of yourself before joining your partner in these exercises? It's hard to engage meaningfully if you are hungry, stressed, or preoccupied. Take the time to nourish your bodies, clear your minds, and set the stage for an enjoyable exchange. (See the Pre-Conversation Checklist on page 50 for some guidance.)
* **Reward yourselves.** Find a mutually rewarding activity that reinforces your connection through this workbook. Perhaps you could prepare a lovely pot of tea, snuggle up on the couch next to the fire, and even give your workbook time a clever name, like "Teatime" or "Our Us Meeting" or "Dialogue Date."
* **Be specific about your end time.** Agree beforehand how long the conversation will last (e.g., 10, 30, or 60 minutes) and then stick to it. The actual length of time doesn't matter as much as agreeing to spend this time together.

This is how we envision our time together:

DAY AND TIME: ______________________________

What we will do before our scheduled time to show up as our best selves:

PARTNER A: ______________________________

____

PARTNER B: ______________________________

____

Our rewarding activity will be: ____________________________________

Our time together will be ________________________________ minutes

Reminder: This Path Is Winding

It's great to dive into these conversations with high hopes—and we think you should. Simply making the time to get to know each other better is a win. But building new habits takes time, so remember that slow and steady wins the race. Here are a few realistic expectations to keep in mind as you embark on the journey of reconnection:

- **Developing awareness of each other's needs and feelings takes practice.** Reconnecting and deepening your connection doesn't happen instantaneously. It is a process that takes time and consistent effort. Becoming more aware of each other's needs and feelings is a skill that requires practice.
- **Strive for progress, not perfection.** There will be moments of progress and setbacks along the way. Understand that perfection isn't the goal. What matters is the effort and intention you both put into nurturing your relationship.
- **Celebrate small wins.** Even showing up for this work and these conversations is a win. Go ahead and give yourself some credit right now. Collecting victories, whether they involve a heartfelt conversation, a shared moment of laughter, or a show of support, contributes to the overall progress in your relationship.

Pre-Conversation Checklist

Before initiating a conversation, it's essential to ensure that the conditions are conducive to a productive, respectful, and meaningful exchange. Here's a checklist to help each of you determine if it's the right time to engage:

1. Am I hungry or physically uncomfortable? If you're hungry or experiencing physical discomfort, your focus may be on those sensations rather than on the conversation. Consider having a snack or addressing your physical needs before proceeding.

2. Am I stressed, overwhelmed, or busy? High levels of stress, feeling overwhelmed, or being busy can hinder effective communication. If you're preoccupied with these concerns, it might be best to reschedule the conversation for a more relaxed time.

3. Is my heart racing or am I feeling anxious? If you're experiencing physical signs of anxiety, like a racing heart or shallow breathing, it may be challenging to engage in a productive conversation. Take a few moments to breathe deeply and regulate your nervous system before proceeding.

4. Am I calm and focused? Being in a calm and focused state is ideal for effective communication. If you're in a relaxed mindset, you're more likely to listen actively and express yourself clearly.

5. Do I have adequate time for this conversation? Ensure that you have enough time for the conversation without feeling rushed. It's important not to initiate a meaningful dialogue when you're pressed for time.

6. Am I open to listening and empathizing? Ask yourself whether you're in a mindset to actively listen and empathize with your partner. If you're too preoccupied with your own thoughts or feelings, it might be better to wait until you're more open and receptive.

7. Have I checked my assumptions and biases? Reflect on any pre-conceived notions or biases that might affect the conversation. If you've noticed biases, it's a good practice to address them or seek to understand your partner's perspective more openly.

Scoring

If you answered no to most of the questions from 1 to 3 and yes to most of the questions from 4 to 7, you're likely in a good mental and emotional state to engage in the conversation. Remain attentive to any signs of tension or discomfort during the exchange. And remember that sometimes the best thing to do is take a break if a conversation begins to veer off track.

If you answered yes to most of the questions from 1 to 3 and no to most of the questions from 4 to 7, it may be best to postpone the conversation and revisit it when you're in a more optimal state for open and effective communication.

Remember that conversations require the right conditions for success. Ensuring that each of you is in an ideal mental and emotional state can significantly enhance the quality and impact of your interactions. Give yourselves time (at least 20 minutes) to reset before you try again. Use those 20 minutes to do something other than think about the relationship, so that you can come back with a clean slate, open to what might come next.

Part 2
LET'S GET TALKING

Welcome to part 2, the heart of your conversation journey, with dozens of relationship-building exercises and conversations designed to strengthen, deepen, and revitalize your marriage. Throughout these chapters, you can anticipate a mixture of joy and reflection. These questions aren't just prompts; they're gateways to rediscovering the qualities that brought you together and uncovering new dimensions of your connection.

Bring that spirit of curiosity with you as you delve into the questions, remembering that the tools you acquired in part 1 are there to support you at any point in your voyage. This curiosity is your compass, guiding you toward deeper understanding and intimacy.

Upon completing part 2, you can expect a more profound connection with each other, as well as a greater sense of fulfillment in your marriage. Meaningful conversations, like the ones you're about to engage in, are the gateway to deep and lasting connection.

CHAPTER 3

Revisiting Our Love Story

In this chapter you'll take a delightful jaunt down memory lane to rediscover the feelings of fondness, passion, optimism, and wonder that initially brought you together. Revisiting these emotions is an essential step in reconnecting and rekindling your love in the present. These conversations serve as a bridge between the past and the present, helping you understand how your love story has evolved while reigniting the spark that's always been at its core.

These topics tap into the purest, most authentic emotions that characterize the early stages of love. By exploring these feelings and memories, you'll enhance your conversations and deepen your connection, providing a powerful foundation for the journey ahead. So let's embark on this adventure and rediscover the magic that has always been a part of your love story.

Falling in Love

Revisiting the initial butterflies, shared laughter, and whispered dreams from your early days can reawaken those magical feelings that made your relationship so energizing. Reliving the magic of your origin story enhances intimacy, encourages vulnerability, and fosters a deeper emotional and physical bond between you and your partner in the present.

Let these conversations ignite the spark, reminding you of the magnetic pull that brought you together in the first place. Aim to rekindle the flames of your desire for each other and remember the magnetic energy that once fueled your connection.

Exercise

1. Create a playlist of songs from the days when you first fell in love to help re-create the emotional landscape of your early relationship. Choose songs that hold sentimental value for you as a couple. Then sit back and listen.

2. As each song plays, reminisce about the emotions and memories tied to that track. Share anecdotes, funny stories, or what you felt during those moments. Afterward, discuss how listening to these songs together made you feel. What memories did your playlist bring back?

Conversation Questions

- What was the moment each of us realized we were falling in love? Was it a grand revelation or a subtle realization?
- If we each had to choose a song that perfectly captures the essence of our early days together, what would it be?

* If our relationship were a book, what genre would it belong to and which literary characters would we compare ourselves to?
* If we could go back to any moment in our early relationship, where would we go and what advice would we give ourselves?
* What role did fate play in our union? Did we actively choose each other? Have our perspectives on this changed over time?
* What dreams or aspirations did we share during the early days of our relationship? How have they evolved over time?
* What quote or piece of wisdom, if any, has guided us through the journey of falling and staying in love?
* What role did humor play in the early days of our relationship? What are our favorite inside jokes or funny memories that still make us laugh?
* Did we ever write each other love letters or notes in the early days? If so, what was the gist of them? Do either of us still have them?

Ritual of Connection

Get creative and re-create one of your first dates. Try to recall as many details as possible. Go to the same place or somewhere like it. Discuss if you remember what each of you was wearing, and dress in the style of clothing you would have worn at that time. Do you recall your first meal together? Eat a meal you would have eaten together back then.

Early Memories Together

Exploring early memories fosters a sense of nostalgia and reminds you of the moments that shaped your connection. These questions invite you to revisit the laughter, challenges, and growth you experienced together. Challenges are inevitable in any relationship, but it's *how* you remember them together that defines your connection today.

Give yourselves permission to be curious about the triumphs *and* the trials of your early times together. Look for the hidden surprises in these memories and allow them to reinforce a richer, more resilient bond that brings you closer.

Exercise

SUPPLIES: paper, ruler, pencils

1. Grab a piece of paper and turn it sideways to create a timeline for your relationship. On the far left, make a mark for the date you met. On the far right, put today's date. Together, choose intervals that make sense to you (a month, a year, five years, 10 years, etc.).
2. Add additional marks and labels that include key milestones and important life moments that shaped your journey together on the timeline. Think through transitions together, location changes, and the cast of characters who came in and out of your life. Make notes about what was going on for you during those periods.
3. Now, from left to right, draw a line representing the ebbs and flows of your relationship across the length of your timeline. A line going up represents the good times. A line going down represents the more challenging periods.

4. Look at your timeline together. Does it have defined phases? What would you call them (e.g., Young & Dumb, the Grind)? Have fun naming the periods of ebb and flow.

Conversation Questions

* What do you remember feeling the first time you told me you loved me? Why did you choose that moment to tell me?
* What sliding door moment could have changed the course of our relationship forever, and what might have been different?
* What is one of the biggest hurdles we overcame as a couple early in our relationship?
* What moment cemented our relationship?
* Which of our previous experiences shaped how we handle adversity as a couple now?
* What strengths do we rely on in each other during hard times?
* What is our proudest accomplishment from those early days as a couple?
* If we were to choose our favorite year as a couple, what year would it be, and why?

Ritual of Connection

Think about what was popular the year you met. Do an internet search together for that decade's pop culture. You can even search what was going on that specific year. As you start recalling what was going on around you during that time (e.g., events, shows, fashion trends, music), share any memories that come to mind, allowing the nostalgia to wash over you.

Revisiting Our Vows

In relationships, growth and change are constants. Revisiting your vows is one way to foster intimacy and renewal during that change. It can serve as a reminder of the enduring love and shared aspirations that bind you together, providing strength and resilience for the future challenges you may face down the road.

It's also fun. Regardless of how much time has passed since they were first spoken, revisiting vows allows you to honor your journey, celebrate your growth, and renew your dedication to your marriage. It's an opportunity to reevaluate your commitments to each other with an earned perspective that isn't present early in a relationship.

Exercise

1. Read your original wedding vows to each other. If they aren't available, write new ones, or do an internet search for "traditional vows."

2. Now reflect on how three of these vows have played out in your life since your wedding day. Has your understanding of these vows evolved over the years? What does each vow mean to you now?

Vow:

What does it mean now?

PARTNER A	PARTNER B

Vow:

What does it mean now?

PARTNER A	PARTNER B

Vow:

What does it mean now?	
PARTNER A	PARTNER B

Vow:

What does it mean now?	
PARTNER A	PARTNER B

Conversation Questions

* Reflecting on our marriage journey, what are some of our favorite moments together, and why do they hold a special place in our hearts?
* What traditions or rituals within our marriage do you hold dear? How do you think these traditions and rituals contribute to our bond?
* What are some of the funniest moments we've shared together as a couple?
* What are some small, everyday things I do that bring you joy? How do these seemingly mundane actions contribute to your happiness?
* What are the meaningful conversations we've had that really stick with each of us? How do these deep, heart-to-heart discussions foster understanding and intimacy in our marriage?
* What successes and triumphs have we experienced during our marriage? How have these successes and triumphs strengthened our connection as a couple?
* During our marriage, what challenges have we experienced that we faced together as a couple? How have we grown stronger as a result?
* What are your favorite ways to show and receive affection? How do these expressions of love deepen our connection and bring joy to our marriage?

Ritual of Connection

Pull out your wedding photos and spend time looking closely at each photo. Try to feel the feelings you had at the time. Take turns sharing stories and thoughts for each photo. Who were you at that time? What wedding traditions were important to you? Who participated in your wedding ceremony? Do you still have relationships with those people? Were certain people missing that you wish were there?

A Foundation of Trust

Trust is the cornerstone of enduring love. This section invites you to explore the process of creating a safe space to be vulnerable and establishing trust early in your relationship. Revisiting the moments when you cultivated trust in each other lays the groundwork for a deeper understanding of your mutual commitment.

When you unravel the threads of honesty, transparency, and accountability, you reinforce the proof of your alliance. Trust-building requires constant care and attention to evolve and affirm a sense of secure attachment and emotional safety—essential ingredients of an intimate connection.

Exercise

1. Every popular fairy tale and rom-com has a similar plot in which the main character finds love after overcoming an insurmountable hardship. While they rely on their own resilience, these characters always have help along the way. Do you remember a specific moment in which your partner showed up for you when you were struggling?
2. Narrate your love story as if it were a romantic comedy, making your partner a central character who helped soften your heart through exchanges of intimacy and trustworthiness. In the end, this character earns the love of the protagonist (you).
3. In the space provided, write a short story in the third person about how two people's love evolved from a moment of shared intimacy and emotional connection. Remember, every good fairy tale begins with "Once upon a time . . ." Take turns adding sentences.

Conversation Questions

- How intuitive is it for you to rely on another person? Do you feel more or less comfortable relying on me?
- What small ways did we build trust initially in our relationship in those first six months?
- What are some historic examples of vulnerability between us?
- What is one of your distinct memories of me showing soft and vulnerable emotions with you? How does this display of emotion make you feel?
- What was your previous belief about making yourself vulnerable to a romantic partner? How did those feelings evolve in our relationship as our love and trust strengthened for each other?
- What are the moments when you felt most secure and safe in our relationship? What specifically reinforced this feeling of security?

Ritual of Connection

Spend an evening watching your favorite romantic comedy together or choose a new one. Eliminate any distractions and snuggle up. As the story plays out, pay attention to how intimacy and trust builds between the lead characters. Pause the movie occasionally to discuss anything that stands out to you.

Our Marriage Model

Do you ever wonder how you formed your definition of "marriage"? For most of us it is understandably from our parents. For Zach, it was also from the sitcoms he watched on TV, forming an idyllic view of relationships from the well-curated families that showed up in his home night after night.

What about you? How did you form your view of relationships? Explore the fascinating topic of how you and your partner formed your unique "marriage model." This section delves into the early influences, role models, and personal values that shaped your perceptions of marriage. Understanding the roots of your individual and shared visions can reveal insights into how and why you made relationship decisions throughout your life.

By exploring the intricacies of your marriage model, you not only gain insight into each other's expectations but also foster open communication about your shared dreams and aspirations. This exploration is key to bringing you closer, aligning your paths, and deepening your bond.

Exercise

Roles within your relationship are rarely explicitly defined, nor are they usually discussed apart from eruptions when expectations aren't met and resentment builds. The roles couples fall into are often ones that were modeled for them in their families and dominant cultures. Relationship roles come with a set pattern of behavior, and when these behaviors align, peace, safety, and harmony can exist.

This exercise helps you clarify responsibilities, expectations, and behavior for specific roles in your relationship. Review the list of roles, and note which of you fills these particular roles, designating yourselves Partner A or Partner B. This isn't an exhaustive list, so feel free to write in any other roles one or both of you might play. Don't overthink it, and don't try to get it sorted just now. Simply note the places where you agree and disagree to bring awareness to the topic.

Adult Child	Cleaner	Nurturer
Adventurer	Disciplinarian	Parent
Caretaker	Fixer	Peacemaker
Chauffeur	Friend	Planner
Cheerleader	Listener	Social Coordinator
Chef	Money Manager	Volunteer

Partner A

Partner B

Conversation Questions

- Who was the best/healthiest model of partnership for you growing up?
- What was the best/worst relationship advice you ever received?
- How do you think your expectations of yourself have changed as our relationship has matured?
- How do you think your expectations of me have changed as our relationship has matured?
- How did your family of origin affect how you developed your view of roles within the family?
- Are there specific cultural values or traditions that inform how you understand specific roles and responsibilities in our relationship?
- Which roles do we each need better clarity and alignment on to reduce tension?
- What is a modern marriage model we can agree is worthy of adoration?

Ritual of Connection

Take turns sharing your first impressions of weddings. Did you see them on television or in the movies? Did you attend any? Now share your first impressions of marriage. Aside from your parents (if they were married), what other examples of marriage can you name? When did you start thinking about your own wedding and your own marriage?

Discovering Intimacy

Many couples think "intimacy" equals "sex." Sex is certainly part of the equation, but intimacy is much more than sex. This section encourages you to explore the intricacies of intimacy within your relationship. You'll be asked to reflect on the moments when you began unraveling the layers of emotional and physical closeness. Exploring the path you took in discovering intimacy fosters a greater understanding of each other's desires, fears, and vulnerabilities.

Delving into this topic ignites the spark of passion by deepening the emotional bond that forms the essence of your partnership. This exploration is a pathway to bringing you closer, enriching the shared narrative of your intimacy and connection.

Exercise

1. Truth or Dare is an age-old game that hinges on the level of risk placed on either revealing oneself emotionally or potentially embarrassing oneself with actions meant to push your level of comfort.

2. Partner A will ask, "Truth or dare?" Partner B chooses whether to reveal something about themselves or engage in a "dare" that deepens your intimacy. For example, you might dare your partner to make at least 30 seconds of eye contact or touch your body in a gently risky way. Or you might ask for the truth of their emotional state or what they hope to gain from this exploration.

3. Limit the game to three to five minutes so each of you gets only two to three turns. (This is not time for an extended session as much as it's an opportunity to surface ideas to explore.) Focus instead on the curiosities and aspirations that inform your thinking about sex and intimacy. The goal is to draw closer through your mutual exploration of this tender topic.

Conversation Questions

* What did you learn about your own pleasure growing up?
* What did you learn about other people's pleasure growing up?
* What was our first intimate exchange with each other?
* What three words would you use to describe your sexuality?
* What is one of your fondest memories of a sexy encounter with me over the entirety of our relationship? What makes this one the fondest?
* Is there an element of risk, fear, or novelty that appeals to you in our expression of sexuality?
* Is there an element of safety and predictability that appeals to you in our expression of sexuality?

Ritual of Connection

Sit or lie together in a comfortable place and tune in to your own bodies. Take a few deep breaths to release any tension you may be bringing to the exercise. Taking turns, describe aloud the physical sensation of being you. Can you feel the temperature on your skin? The earth supporting your body? What is your heart doing? Do you have any aches and pains? Does any part feel especially relaxed?

Overcoming Hurdles

While the early phases of a relationship are usually full of exciting adventures, they almost always include their share of obstacles. Here you'll reflect on the challenges you faced as a couple and how you navigated through them. Delving into these experiences not only deepens your understanding of each other but also reinforces your shared perseverance and unity that emerged from adversity.

Reflecting on shared challenges—and especially how you overcame them—can bring you closer together. By exploring how you overcame hurdles and creating a narrative of shared triumphs, you reinforce your identity as a resilient couple who can handle adversity.

Exercise

SUPPLIES: scrap paper and pens

1. On your scrap paper, brainstorm the challenges, adversity, mistakes, and regrettable incidents of your past as a couple. Take turns writing your past challenges until you have an exhaustive list, spanning multiple pieces of paper.

2. When couples tell us the history of their relationships, their stories are often labeled with titles like "The time we lived with your mom" or "When we went bankrupt and walked away from our house" or "The first time you broke your foot." Also use this as an opportunity to take personal accountability by reflecting on personal decisions and behaviors that also impacted your relationship (e.g., "Quitting my job without talking to you first," "I stopped paying attention to scheduling emails and dropped the ball," or "Traveled too much for work").

3. Here comes the fun part! Purposely and ceremoniously crumple the pages into balls and toss them into a fire. Burn, baby, burn those

pages to ashes! Doing this represents your ability to move forward from your hardships. The ashes are evidence that you have overcome these moments of adversity, bad behavior, mistakes, and pain.

Caution: To prevent a need to write "The time we burned the house down," be sure to find a safe place to build a fire, such as a fireplace, firepit, or charcoal grill.

Conversation Questions

- What is one of the most challenging experiences you've dealt with so far in your life?
- If you could redo one of the years of our relationship to navigate challenges differently, which would you choose, and why?
- How do you typically handle adversity? Do you put your head down and plow through? Collapse and drown in emotion? Take each moment as it comes and feel the pain and the delight?
- What is one of the best examples of when we thrived by locking arms and persevering through a tough time together?
- How do we typically recover and reunite after hardship?
- What regrettable incidents of the past still need our or my attention? (Be gentle with this one; you're not trying to solve it, just surface it.)
- What do you need to heal the trauma of the past?

Ritual of Connection

This ritual is called "tour of scars." From head to toe and from large to small, take your partner on a tour of your physical scars. Share the stories that go along with how you remember getting these scars. Some scars are worth the pain and discomfort you endured and can serve as visual reminders that strength and beauty can come from hardship. Talk about this too. Afterward, switch roles.

Sliding versus Deciding

Consider the difference between sliding and deciding. Sliding implies inevitable inertia (e.g., "We should move in together since my lease is expiring"). Deciding implies much more intention (e.g., "Let's move in together"). This section delves into the conscious choices and pivotal moments that shaped your shared journey.

In this reflection you not only gain insights into your shared history but also expose opportunities for intentional growth. Unraveling the dynamics of sliding into decisions versus making intentional choices deepens your understanding of your journey while prompting meaningful conversations about the choices that led you here. It also sheds light on how you may approach future decisions.

Exercise

Go back and look at the timeline you created in "Early Memories Together" (see page 58). This timeline of your relationship outlines significant moments in your relationship. Review each important event and discuss whether each moment came by way of sliding or deciding. Do you notice any trends? What role did emotional safety play in your sliding versus deciding in any of these events?

Conversation Questions

- What factors might impact us when it comes to sliding into major life decisions versus making intentional life decisions?
- Do we fundamentally differ in how we make major relationship decisions?
- What differences do we see in the way each of us makes decisions?
- What comes to mind when you hear the word "compromise"?

* How are we at sharing power in the decision-making process?
* Do you feel open to my influence when we are making joint decisions?
* What is our process for making big decisions?
* What is our process for making small decisions?

Ritual of Connection

What's one decision you'll need to make within the next six months? Aim to finalize your decision today. When choosing something to decide on here, avoid trying to solve a perpetual problem. Instead, choose something that's easily solvable. Some examples include where you'll spend the next holiday, whether to purchase a new mattress, or if you'll renew your gym membership. Use this as an opportunity to be intentional about checking something off your list.

Balancing Me & We

Take a journey of self-discovery within the context of your relationship as you explore the delicate dance between individuality and unity. This exploration invites you to consider the balance between independence and interdependence by highlighting the moments when you transitioned from "you and me" to a beautifully entwined "we."

Understanding how your unique personality traits contribute to your shared identity not only deepens your connection but also fortifies the bonds of togetherness. By delving into the celebration of both the "me" and the "we" within your unique partnership, you strengthen your connection, creating a space where your individual identities flourish on your shared path.

Exercise

1. Look at the Venn diagram and choose who will be Partner A and who will be Partner B.
2. Take turns brainstorming your unique personality characteristics, hobbies, values, and friends, and write it all down in the section of your circle that does *not* overlap with your partner's.
3. Now brainstorm as a team the aspects of your "we-ness" that represent parts of your life that are shared and cherished within your partnership, then write them in the section that overlaps.

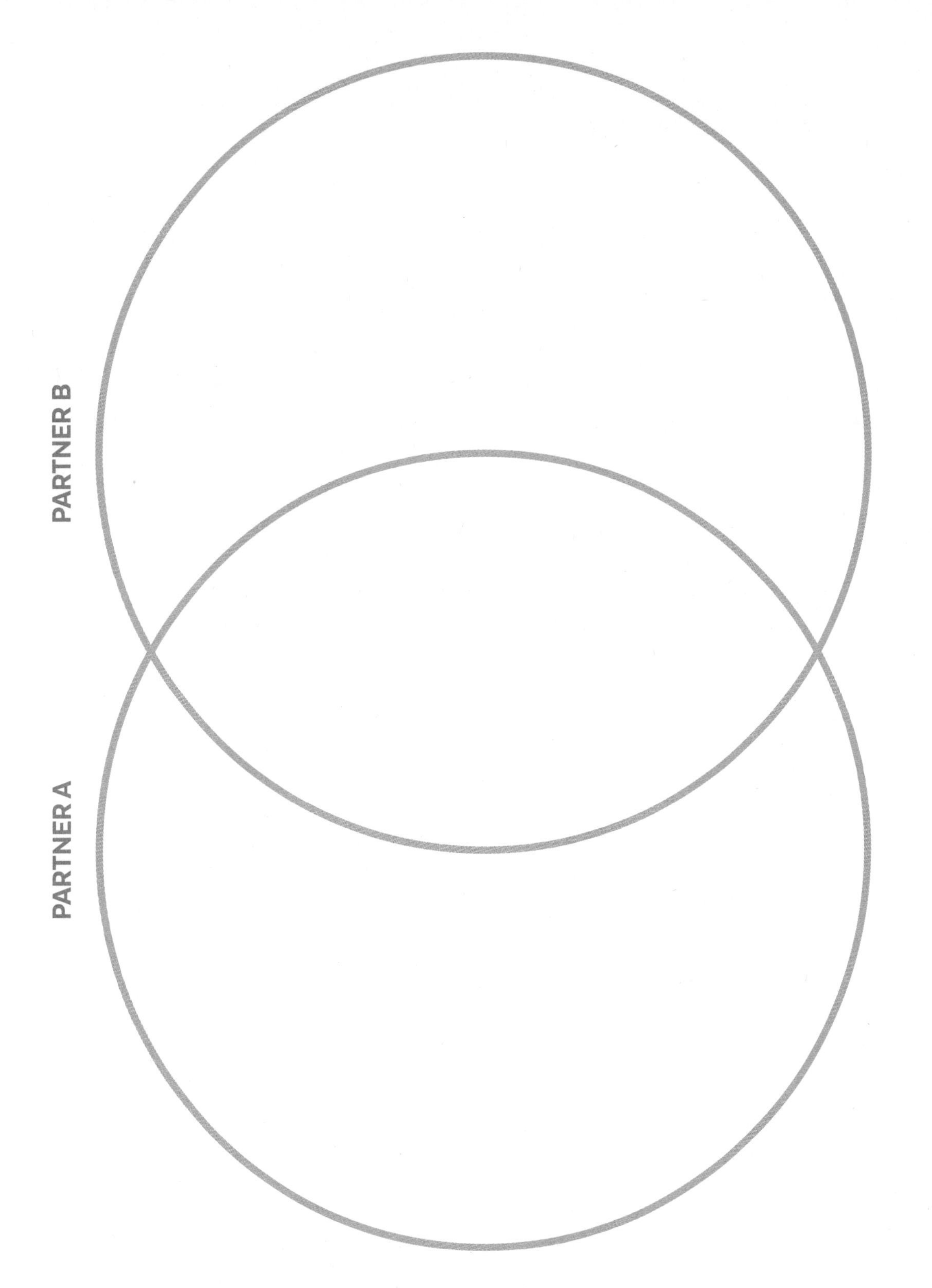
PARTNER B
PARTNER A

Conversation Questions

* How does your sense of individuality compare to my sense of individuality?
* If we had done this Venn diagram when we first partnered, what would it have looked like?
* Has my influence on you changed you in any way as far as your likes/dislikes, hobbies, and friendships?
* Are there any changes we would like to make to our diagram today?
* What might we consider adding to our shared space to deepen our connection?
* Do you feel comfortable or uncomfortable about merging more into a sense of "we"? If uncomfortable, what may be the reason?

Ritual of Connection

Stand, facing each other, close enough to reach out for an embrace. Plant your feet firmly on the ground. Now equally lean in, meeting in the middle. Aim to not fall off balance by putting too much weight on your partner or taking on your partner's weight. Wrap your arms around each other and hold for at least 30 seconds. Try to synchronize your breath. End your embrace with a squeeze as a gentle cue to disengage.

CHAPTER 4

Where We Came From

In this chapter you'll look back on your early years before you met your partner, sifting through the moments that made each of you uniquely you. From there you'll consider how these experiences and values brought you together and shaped your marriage.

It's not uncommon for conversations about our history to bring up intense feelings. Old wounds might resurface like a stubborn weed you thought you'd plucked. Working through the rituals of connection and exercises first will tee up your conversations for intimacy, support, and understanding. As always, take it one question at a time, skipping any that you need time to process or are not ready to visit. Remember to trust that everything from your past makes you who you are today. So let's gather our gardening tools and get to work tending this fertile ground.

Family Dynamics

Our families of origin gave us the first building blocks through which to understand ourselves and the world. Exploring these dynamics brings deeper understanding to each person's roots, while prompting new inquiry around how these early influences still appear today. By delving into family-of-origin history, there is an opportunity to find clarity, forgiveness, and release.

Consider this section as the start of a pathway that runs through your early experiences to this current moment. This pathway is designed to bring you closer through a shared understanding of the familial patterns that help define each of you and your marriage.

Exercise

Many of our expectations and appreciations of "normal" come from our family-of-origin stories. In this exercise you will investigate who and what represented "normal" to you. As you reflect on the people who shaped you, feel free to do a little storytelling. Pay attention to any surprises that show up for you and don't forget to be thankful for those who helped you get here.

	PARTNER A	PARTNER B
When I had emotional needs, I turned toward:		
The relationship I had with my siblings was:		
When I was young I remember feeling this way toward my father/mother/caretaker:		
My parents' relationship was:		
My parents' financial situation was:		

	PARTNER A	PARTNER B
One value that was most prized in my family was:		
What did I want from my mother/father/caretaker that I never received:		
In my family of origin, expressing emotions was:		
The atmosphere of my daily family life was:		
Religion and spirituality were viewed as:		

Conversation Questions

* In what ways do you see echoes of your parents' relationship in our relationship?
* What lessons—positive or challenging—have you brought forward from your parents' relationship?
* How do you think your parents would describe their relationship?
* How do your relationships with your siblings impact how you think about relationships or family dynamics? If you are an only child, how did this shape your view of the nuclear family?
* Which family quirks—funny, endearing, or challenging—have become part of our shared language, and how do they contribute to our own unique family dynamic?
* Have any of our family-of-origin anecdotes become parables in our marriage, offering guidance or a good laugh during challenging times?
* In what ways do the roles of matriarchs and patriarchs in our families influence our own leadership and decision-making as a couple?
* What aspects of your family-of-origin dynamics do you hope to pass down to future generations?
* What aspects of your family-of-origin dynamics do you consciously aim to transform or evolve?

Ritual of Connection

Set a date night to cozy up with each other on the couch and pull out all the family photos you have from your childhoods. Take turns reflecting on the people and roles each family member played in the family dynamic. Discuss the important events and rituals these photographs memorialize and how they served as markers for your growth and development as a couple.

Role of Spirituality/Religion

Spiritual intimacy can be an essential part of a couple's connection. For some people, spirituality is connected to a faith tradition. For others, it's more universal. Perhaps spirituality is more important to one of you than it is to the other. Or perhaps it's simply not a value. If this section doesn't resonate, feel free to skip it.

By delving into the intricacies of your spiritual landscape, you can strengthen your connection, creating a new space for shared rituals, profound discussions, and a deeper sense of unity. These conversations can foster spiritual intimacy and help connect you to the more transcendent dimensions of your unique partnership.

Exercise

1. For this exercise, set aside time to each write individually about your spiritual upbringings and what has or hasn't changed in your adult lives.

2. As you reflect on your experiences of "the sacred," divide your reflections into chunks of 5 to 10 years. What was your experience of the first 10 years as a child? How about 11 to 20 years old? Did it shift in your twenties? Your thirties? Beyond? The goal is to create a personal spiritual timeline to inform your conversation.

Conversation Questions

- What do you see as the differences between religion and spirituality?
- How have your beliefs changed over time, if at all?
- What was the first spiritual community you felt connected to?
- How do you feel spirituality relates to marriage? Has this changed since our wedding day?
- Is there any part of spirituality you feel belongs just to you? In other words, what aspects of your spirituality do you prefer to practice alone?
- Does spirituality have anything to do with personal growth? If so, what?
- How might we deepen our shared spiritual practice?
- Would we like to do some kind of daily devotion, prayer, meditation, or intention-setting together?

Ritual of Connection

Do you remember a prayer, motto, or quote from childhood that brought you a sense of comfort or peace during hard times? Share it with your partner and describe how those words have served throughout your life thus far. Are the prayers, mottoes, or quotes that you each hold in your hearts similar or different? In what way?

Emotional Bonds

Some of our most enduring relationship strategies form even before we leave the crib. This is the basis for "attachment theory," proposed and developed by psychologist and psychiatrist John Bowlby in the 1960s and 1970s. It explores the nature of emotional bonds between individuals, particularly the attachment between child and primary caregiver.

In this section you'll reflect on the bonds formed during your youngest years. Learning about early attachment can deepen your self-awareness and help you bring empathy to your partner's emotional landscape. Understanding your partner's patterns of safety, as well as your own, especially in conflict, creates space for vulnerability, nonjudgment, and connection.

Exercise

1. Use the following chart to familiarize yourself with the four major attachment styles. From the descriptions, note whether you recognize yourself in one of these attachment styles.

SECURE	ANXIOUS
I tend to have stable, fulfilling connections and healthy boundaries with others.	I tend to have high anxiety levels and relationships that lack trust or thrive on "the chase."
AVOIDANT	**DISORGANIZED**
I tend to have more distant relationships that sometimes stem from a fear of commitment.	I tend to have high anxiety and avoidance and am often drawn to people with similar energy.

2. Regardless of which style you think is your default, independently think about your answers to each of the following questions. Then look back at the chart and determine in which quadrant your response might fall. This should help you gain some clarity around your typical attachment style. This isn't a quiz; rather, it's self-exploration, so just explore.

   A. What's your reaction if your partner expresses a need for space or independence?

   B. Do you tend to withdraw or seek closeness in stressful situations?

   C. Were there any patterns in your past relationships in how you approached intimacy and trust?

   D. How do you typically respond when you perceive a threat to the relationship?

   E. How comfortable are you with being vulnerable?

Conversation Questions

- When did you feel particularly close and connected to me?
- In what ways do you recognize your attachment style showing up in our relationship?
- When we argue or disagree, do you tend to seek closeness or distance?
- How do our attachment styles interact with each other?
- What is something I can do to help you feel safe and secure in our relationship?
- How can I support you when you need independence without feeling distant?
- Are there specific behaviors or actions that signal to you when I'm feeling distant or overwhelmed?

Ritual of Connection

This ritual of saying yes to your partner's bid for connection is a surefire way to build trust. Sit across from each other, eyes closed. Partner A says Partner B's name aloud, making a bid for connection. Partner B responds with a gentle, clear yes. Repeat this pattern for 15 seconds, and then switch roles. Pay attention to how your body feels when it gets a clear, direct response to your bid for connection.

Leaving Home for the First Time

Do you remember your first sleepover? Or when you left for summer camp or got dropped off at your freshman dorm? Life is punctuated with significant moments of stepping out on one's own. This section invites you to revisit the pivotal moments when you ventured out into the world independently.

Leaving home is a major milestone and the first step toward becoming a grown-up. Delving into the emotions and experiences of leaving home gives you a deeper appreciation of each other's journeys. Understanding the initial context of your independence is foundational to appreciating how each of you shows up in your grown-up relationship today.

Exercise

While aspects of our personality are unchanging, we are human-growth machines that stretch, grow, and adapt with every new experience. Leaving home for the first time is a pivotal core memory and is often the first significant moment of independence in our lives.

Set a timer for five minutes. One partner goes at a time. As you respond to the prompts, recall how you felt and which aspect of your personality was most pronounced.

PARTNER A

My memory of leaving home for the first time:

Describe a later memory that stands out as a moment of declared independence. Reflect on your motivations and feelings during this time. How did you navigate the newfound aspect of independence? How was this experience different from leaving home for the first time?

PARTNER B

My memory of leaving home for the first time:

Describe a later memory that stands out as a moment of declared independence. Reflect on your motivations and feelings during this time. How did you navigate the newfound aspect of independence? How was this experience different from leaving home for the first time?

Conversation Questions

- How do you define "independence"?
- Does independence rank high on your list of values?
- How has your desire for independence changed over time?
- What novel experiences have we each experienced separately over the course of our relationship?
- In what way have these experiences encouraged you to be a better person and better partner?
- What role does interdependence play in our relationship, and how does it differ from independence?
- How can we support each other's individual growth and independence while maintaining our connection and partnership?

Ritual of Connection

Take a stroll down memory lane together, sharing stories about places significant to each other's upbringing and how they shaped your sense of independence. Then, choose something new to try together and make a commitment to explore this shared experience. You can plan an outdoor adventure or challenge yourselves with hiking a difficult trail or completing a ropes course. As you engage in this experience, pay attention to moments of independence and collaboration and what feelings come up for you.

Friendships, Then & Now

Exploring our earliest friendships can tell us a lot about what we look for in others as well as what qualities we bring to the table. This section invites you to reflect on the relationships that shaped your individual social constructs and influenced your relationship today.

Exploring the dynamics of your friendships over the years together deepens your understanding of each other's social worlds. By delving into the intricacies of friendships, then and now, you'll create a space for shared stories, mutual support, and a deeper appreciation of the ever-evolving social tapestry that binds you together and to your community.

Exercise

1. Look at the diagrams of the concentric circles; there's one for each of you. These circles represent the relationships in your life (e.g., your partner, members of your family of origin, friends, colleagues, counselors, teachers, neighbors).

2. Spend a few moments thinking about the significant people in your life and write their names where you feel they belong in the circle, with the inner circle being those with whom you are most intimate and the outer circle being those who are more removed. The closer you place the person to the center circle, the more intimate the relationship is.

3. When complete, share your circles. If either of you have questions, discuss your reasoning.

PARTNER A

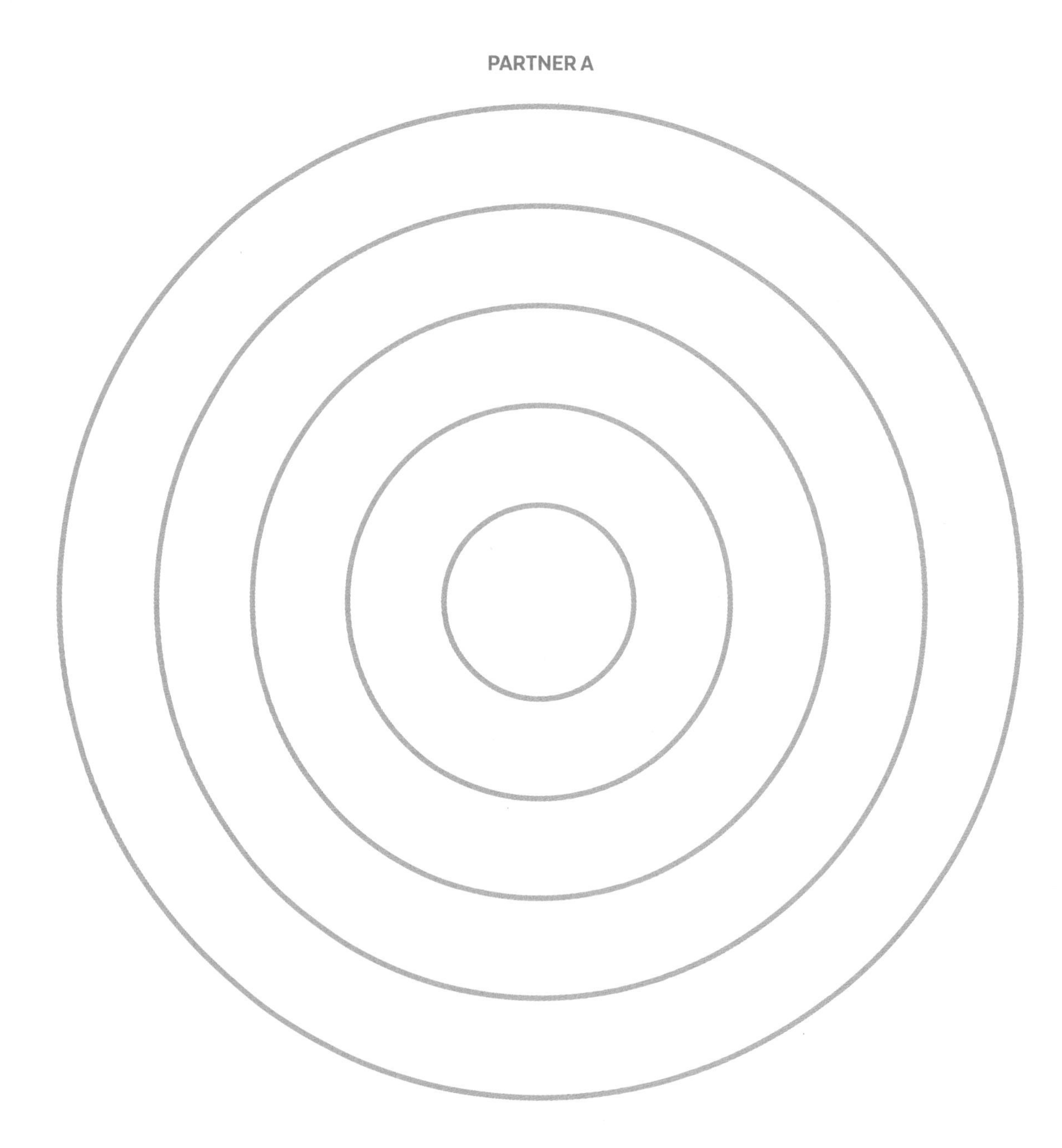

PARTNER B

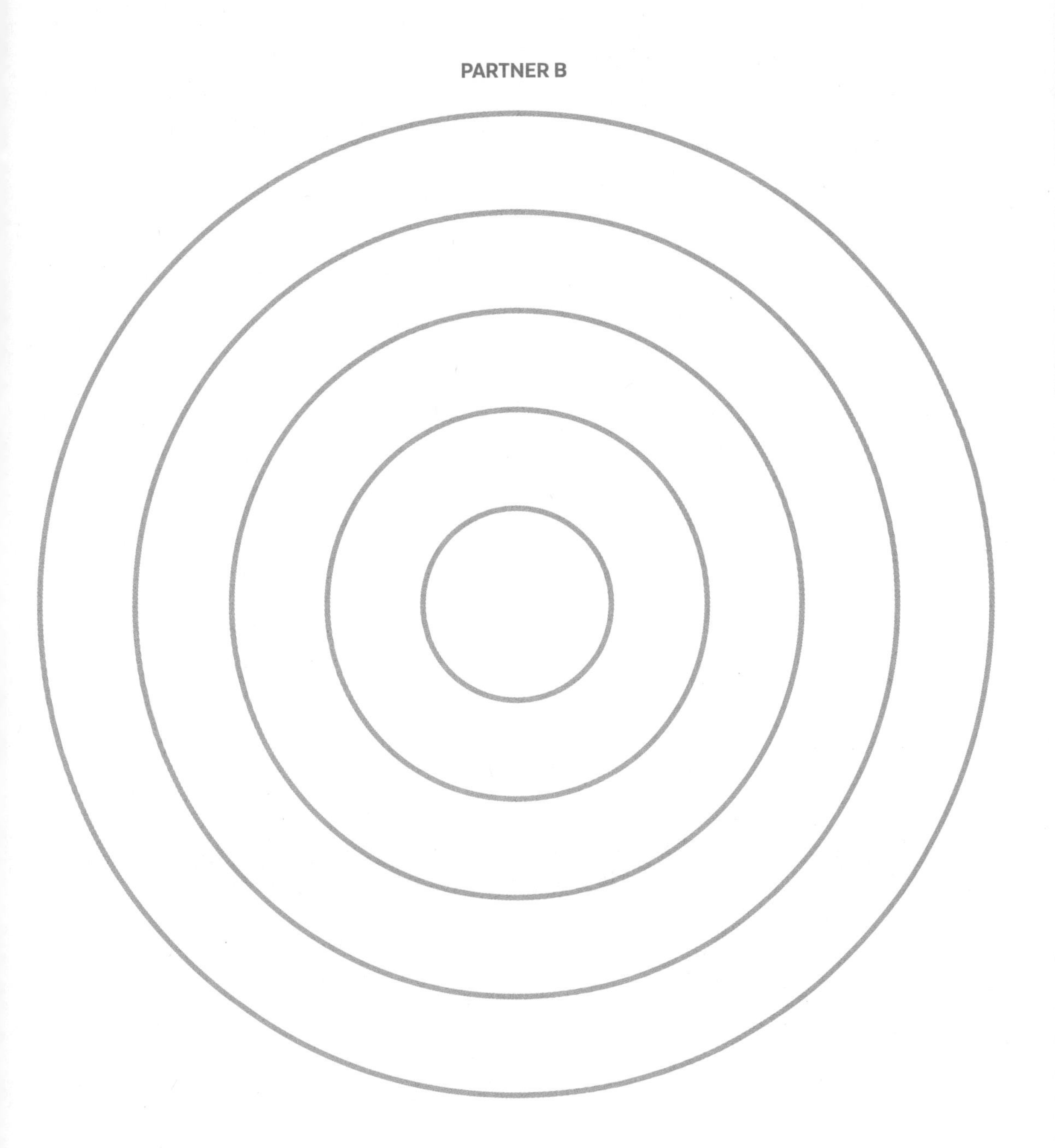

Conversation Questions

* If a particular friend and you were characters in a coming-of-age novel, what adventure and/or lesson would the last chapter recount?
* How would you describe your grade-school friendships? Do you see any similarities with your current friends?
* If your experiences with friends as a teenager had a soundtrack, what songs would be on it? How do those songs encapsulate that time in your life?
* What role did you play in group projects at school? In what ways do those dynamics play out in our relationship?
* Were your experiences at school dances awkward or magical? How did those moments shape your relationship to vulnerability and intimacy?
* How did you navigate conflicts or disagreements in your early friendships? What lessons did you learn about apology and forgiveness?
* If your fourth-grade self could give you friendship advice, what pearls of wisdom would they share?
* How do you navigate digital friendships and connections? What role does technology play in your relationship dynamics?
* How would you describe our friendship as a couple, and what are your favorite parts?

Ritual of Connection

Gather some old photos of each of you with your friends. Look at each image together and take turns sharing stories related to the photo. Name specific people and the events and themes connected to those friendships that you're grateful for. Allow this to foster a deeper understanding of how these relationships helped form who you are today.

Playtime

Relationships take work but also a fair amount of play. *How* you play also says a lot about how you approach the work. This section invites you to reflect on the games and activities you engaged in before you met each other.

By exploring the games and activities that lit each of you up when you were younger, you'll be in a better position to understand how to meet each other's needs today and maybe even have some ideas for adventures you'd like to embark on together. Even if you had completely different ideas of playtime as children, you can still pursue shared play as a couple.

Exercise

Many couples who seek therapy tend to be more individual in their pursuit of play, pleasure, and restoration as time goes on. Reminiscing on what you enjoyed as children can spark ideas for what you might enjoy doing together. For example, did one of you enjoy coloring as a child? If so, maybe you can take a painting class together. If one of you enjoyed playing a sport, see if there's a game or a couples team you can join.

PARTNER A'S CHILDHOOD GAMES AND ACTIVITIES	SHARED CHILDHOOD GAMES AND ACTIVITIES	PARTNER B'S CHILDHOOD GAMES AND ACTIVITIES

Conversation Questions

- Are there any activities on our lists we would be willing to try as adults?
- Is there a grown-up version of what we used to do that we can do now?
- What is something we both used to do that we thought was a lot of fun?
- When and why did we stop participating in these types of games and activities?
- What common themes are present in the games and activities we enjoyed as kids (e.g., outdoor versus inside, teams/group play versus solo play, adventure, creativity)?
- How was play modeled for us when we were growing up? In what ways does this ring true (or untrue) for us today?

Ritual of Connection

Think back to a favorite childhood game and introduce your partner to it—and then just play for the sake of playing. For example, Laura's favorite childhood game was capture-the-flag, so she and her husband invited several neighborhood families to participate in this rowdy game. Though their team lost to the opposition, the experience was bonding and refreshing.

Trauma & Coping

By exploring the nuanced terrain of past trauma and the coping strategies you learned, you're not just revisiting old wounds; you're forging a path toward deeper healing, understanding, and connection.

This section invites you to engage in conversations that transcend trauma, creating a space where vulnerability becomes a bridge to intimacy. By openly discussing your past challenges and coping mechanisms, you cultivate an environment of empathy, understanding, and support. This isn't merely an exercise in reflection; it's a shared commitment to healing and growth. This dialogue should be one of compassion, shared strength, and an unwavering dedication to each other's well-being.

Exercise

Vulnerability is accessible only in safety. To access your vulnerability, you'll need to create an agreement to abide by when discussing hard topics. This exercise helps you build a framework to follow during conversations that may stir up big emotions. Read and discuss the prompt for each of the five areas. Write your agreement in the space provided.

Space: What kind of environment will we have hard conversations in? Some couples enjoy being on long nature walks, while others agree to have hard conversations on a specific couch in their home. (The bedroom should be saved for other uses.)

____

____

____

____

____

Timing: Does the day, time, and duration that you worked out in the exercise on page 48 work for the more difficult conversations you'll be having? If not, what works better? What about the duration? Might you need more time but not so much time that you'll feel burned out?

DAY: ____________ TIME: ____________ DURATION: ____________

Boundaries: What specific boundaries do you need in place to keep the conversation productive and safe? Do you commit to maintaining a respectful tone and volume, refraining from curse words or superlatives ("always" and "never"), and minimizing criticism and defensiveness? These are only examples; include any specific boundaries each of you needs to reinforce safety.

____

____

____

____

____

Self-soothing: Self-soothing behaviors help calm and regulate the nervous system. While feelings and emotions are wonderful, there's a point when emotions are so big that they can interrupt our ability to show up for tough conversations and be an active and compassionate listener. What techniques will each of you use to help yourselves calm down if you get activated?

____

____

____

____

____

____

Taking space: Even the most practiced couples may need to take a break from each other (for at least 20 minutes) when they get activated before they resume connection. In the space provided, brainstorm how you'll know when it's time to take a break. For example, using a safe word will indicate it's time for a break. Also, jot down what each of you can do during this break to reset your body and brain to return to loving connection.

____

____

____

____

____

____

____

Conversation Questions

- When did you feel powerless, and what tools did you have to cope with the aftermath of that experience?
- What message would you like to have heard back then from your older self?
- What does feeling "triggered" look like to you?
- When you feel triggered, what physical or verbal cues do you display that I can look out for to better nurture you in those moments?
- Do you have any symbolic souvenirs from your journey through life that hold particular significance, especially when it comes to overcoming adversity?
- In times of vulnerability, who are the people in your support system who uniquely protect your peace of mind?
- How do people in your support system contribute to the resilience of our relationship?
- When you feel overwhelmed by a past memory, how would you like me to support you?
- Would you like me to ask you more about challenging times, or do you prefer I wait until you invite me to talk about it?

Ritual of Connection

To start difficult conversations from a place of safety and calm, breathe in and out slowly for five minutes. Taking control of your breath this way calms your mind and nervous system. It can also serve as an anchor in the storm of emotions that often accompany hard conversations. If the conversation stirs up fear responses in you, remember you can always come back to your breath. If needed, however, take a break until you're ready to return.

Roles, Rules & Responsibilities

Every relationship contains assumptions about roles and responsibilities that are often adopted from what we learned growing up. Here you'll explore how unspoken agreements influence the breakdown of responsibility in your home, and how these roles shape—and perhaps limit—your connection. Delving into the intricacies of these agreements isn't just about clarifying expectations; it's about proactively choosing the direction and quality of your interaction.

By openly discussing roles, unspoken rules, and responsibilities, you create a space for mutual understanding and collaboration. Remember, it's not merely a conversation about duties; it's a dynamic exploration that strengthens the foundations of your relationship, paving the way for deeper connection and growth.

Exercise

1. Fill out this responsibility audit individually without looking at the other person's answers (two copies are provided). Check off who is responsible; if it's a shared responsibility, check off both. Then rank how satisfied you are with the current arrangement on a scale of 1 to 5, with 1 being mostly dissatisfied.

2. Afterward, compare your answers, paying special attention to your discrepancies. Note whether these are responsibilities you took on because of what you saw growing up.

PARTNER A

	PARTNER A'S RESPONSIBILITY	PARTNER B'S RESPONSIBILITY	SATISFACTION RATING
Bathrooms, cleaning			
Bedroom, tidying			
Bedtime routine (for kids, if any)			
Car care			
Childcare/elder care at home (if applicable)			
Dishwashing			
Family social coordination			
Financial tasks			
Food planning			
Food prep/cooking			
Garbage/recycling			
Grocery shopping			
House repairs			

PARTNER A

	PARTNER A'S RESPONSIBILITY	PARTNER B'S RESPONSIBILITY	SATISFACTION RATING
Laundry			
Lawn care			
Making travel plans			
Medical appointments (scheduling/attending with children or aging parents)			
Pet care/vet appointments (if applicable)			
Preparation for events, activities, and holidays			
School communication (if applicable)			
Shopping for kids, arranging activities, birthday parties, etc. (if applicable)			
Transporting family members to appointments, activities, shopping, etc.			
Vacuuming/sweeping			
Work for wages			

PARTNER B

	PARTNER A'S RESPONSIBILITY	PARTNER B'S RESPONSIBILITY	SATISFACTION RATING
Bathrooms, cleaning			
Bedroom, tidying			
Bedtime routine (for kids, if any)			
Car care			
Childcare/elder care at home (if applicable)			
Dishwashing			
Family social coordination			
Financial tasks			
Food planning			
Food prep/cooking			
Garbage/recycling			
Grocery shopping			
House repairs			

PARTNER B

	PARTNER A'S RESPONSIBILITY	PARTNER B'S RESPONSIBILITY	SATISFACTION RATING
Laundry			
Lawn care			
Making travel plans			
Medical appointments (scheduling/attending with children or aging parents)			
Pet care/vet appointments (if applicable)			
Preparation for events, activities, and holidays			
School communication (if applicable)			
Shopping for kids, arranging activities, birthday parties, etc. (if applicable)			
Transporting family members to appointments, activities, shopping, etc.			
Vacuuming/sweeping			
Work for wages			

Conversation Questions

* What did you find surprising about the responsibility exercise?
* What additional responsibilities do we each manage that aren't on this list?
* Which specific roles and responsibilities might we have modeled after our families of origin?
* Which roles and responsibilities are modeled after our culture and/or society?
* Which responsibilities do you like the least? Why?
* Which individual tasks would you like more recognition for?
* Going forward, how would you like to receive appreciation and recognition for your contributions? What's one thing I can do this week to make this list feel more balanced?
* On a higher level, what would we each like to see moving forward?

Ritual of Connection

Many responsibilities we shoulder go unnoticed, with little to no praise or appreciation. Instead, make a bid for some well-deserved ooohs and aaahs from your partner. For example, Zach spent an afternoon putting up outdoor Christmas lights and invited his wife outside for the grand reveal. Being clear on the assignment, Rebecca enthusiastically clapped with vocal ooohs and aaahs to acknowledge Zach's hard work. Take turns inviting your partner to recognize your efforts with enthusiasm.

Cultural Connections

Exploring the nuances of your cultural heritages can lead to a profound connection around how your inherited stories and lived experiences contribute to the richness of your marriage.

This section invites you to engage in conversations that delve into the traditions, values, stories, and experiences that have shaped your identity. You'll consider cultural roots through a new lens and wonder aloud about their influence on how you approach love, family, and everyday life. This is a transformative dialogue that fosters an entirely new way of thinking about what makes *you* as individuals and as a couple.

Exercise

Celebrations from weddings to weekly family dinners are often packed full of cultural meaning and tradition. For each prompt, discuss how you may have honored that tradition in your culture. Fill in what each of you feels is significant. As you do so, consider whether there are any traditions you would like to deepen as a unified expression of your shared culture as a couple. The list isn't comprehensive; consider any other celebrations that are meaningful to you and your backgrounds.

PARTNER A

Births: ______________________________

____

Coming of age: ______________________________

____

First menses: ______________________________

____

Marriage: ______________________________

____

Wedding anniversary: ______________________________

____

Death: ______________________________

____

Honoring ancestors: ______________________________

____

Retirement: ______________________________

____

Gratitude practices: ______________________________

____

Honoring a higher power/religious practices: ______________________________

____

PARTNER B

Births: ______________________________

____

Coming of age: ______________________________

____

First menses: ______________________________

____

Marriage: ______________________________

____

Wedding anniversary: ______________________________

____

Death: ______________________________

____

Honoring ancestors: ______________________________

____

Retirement: ______________________________

____

Gratitude practices: ______________________________

____

Honoring a higher power/religious practices: ______________________________

____

Conversation Questions

* How does your experience of cultural traditions impact your values?
* Have you adopted or rejected any specific values because of my cultural traditions?
* What is the specific role of men and women in your culture? Are there any stereotypes?
* What early messages did you receive regarding the role of children, adults, and elders in the community?
* How does your background impact your sense of safety and value in the world?
* Does your background play a role in your confidence or self-worth?
* What is your favorite story or legend from your culture?
* What role do cooking and baking play in your culture? Have you carried on those traditions?
* Are there any proverbs or sayings you grew up hearing that offer wisdom about life?
* What is considered respectful and disrespectful in your culture?

Ritual of Connection

Look around right now to see if you can each point out a symbol in your surroundings that represents your culture. These symbols (e.g., clothing, art, trinkets, statues) somehow represent the beliefs, values, mindsets, and practices of any group of people you identify with. As you scan, discuss the ways these various parts of your identity live in and shape your environment.

CHAPTER 5

Who Are We Now?

One of our favorite roles as therapists is detective: asking questions, uncovering clues, and testing theories. It's satisfying to be curious about someone in a way that uncovers previously unspoken truths, desires, and fears. Human relationships (and life) are baked in mystery, and this chapter is where you'll throw on your own detective hat, investigating the inner world of your partner as they exist today.

It's a skill to play detective with the ones we love. One clue is to choose curiosity over judgment—over and over. Remember, your partner isn't a suspect. They're a witness to their own life and yours. The hard truth is that if we don't gain a clear understanding of the present moment, we'll have little say in the next one. So grab your magnifying glass and open yourself to uncovering the wonders of your present-day partner, yourself, and your relationship ecosystem.

Individual Hobbies & Interests

What hobbies light up your days, and how do they shape your perspective on life? Openly discussing your current interests creates a space for a deeper understanding of what makes you tick. By investigating these themes, you'll gain a deeper insight into the ways you can bring joy and energy into each other's lives.

When you can support and encourage your partner's passions, you also create space for them to recharge in a way that allows them to return to the relationship with renewed attention and intention. And perhaps learning what makes your partner tick and why will give you a deeper appreciation of yourself.

Exercise

1. Sit facing each other and take turns naming one of your current hobbies or interests. Write it down and share why it brings you joy and how it adds value to your life.

2. Choose one hobby or interest from each list and try to create a new shared hobby that combines your passions. This is your "hobby fusion" project. For instance, if one of you enjoys cooking and the other loves painting, try a culinary art project. Create a shared goal for the project and identify common ways to support each other in achieving this goal.

CURRENT HOBBIES

PARTNER A	PARTNER B

OUR SHARED HOBBY

Conversation Questions

- If our relationship were a museum showcasing our shared interests and passions, what would the different exhibits say about our relationship overall?
- In the novel of our relationship, how would our shared hobbies and interests inform and affect the overall plot?
- If our relationship were a podcast, which of our hobbies would be good recurring segments? What would we want our audience to learn?
- How do your artistic and/or intellectual pursuits help you feel more present and connected in our relationship?
- Which of your hobbies offers you a sense of peace and self-reflection?
- In what ways do your hobbies act as therapeutic outlets in your pursuit of self-discovery?
- Which pursuits in particular enhance our shared time together?

Ritual of Connection

Create a mini vision board on a piece of construction paper or poster board that highlights some of your shared and individual passions. You can cut out pictures from magazines if you'd like, but it isn't necessary. You can draw symbols and jot down relevant words that represent the hobbies/interests you aspire to explore together or simply support the other person doing. Hang it somewhere you'll both see it.

Work

As kids, our concept of work is often limited to Halloween costumes: firefighter, doctor, barista, wizard. Enter financial responsibility, and the world becomes much more nuanced. Our vocation says a lot about who we are and how we organize our priorities. It also speaks to our overall aspirations and life challenges.

This section invites you to delve into the intricacies of how you spend your time—whether that's on-site or remote (or a combination). You'll investigate your ambitions and any hurdles that keep you from a life of satisfaction. You'll also examine how your personal and professional paths intersect and influence the present landscape of your marriage.

Exercise

Many factors go into your occupational endeavors: personal experience, educational background, personality, skills, labor market, values, interests, and family obligations, to name a few. Throughout your lifetime, you'll likely experience everything from your first under-the-table pocket money to an array of full-time, part-time, and/or domestic roles that drive your daily experience until (and beyond) retirement.

With new life circumstances, your values may change. This exercise helps each of you clarify how your values relate to how your time is spent.

On a scale of 1 to 5 (1 strongly agree, 2 moderately agree, 3 neutral, 4 moderately disagree, 5 strongly disagree), note how true these statements are for you.

It is important for me to have a vocation that...

	PARTNER A	PARTNER B
Provides a sense of independence (e.g., make my own decisions and set my own schedules)		
Includes some level of competition		
Amounts to a high level of respect, recognition, and status in my community or industry		
Requires leadership		
Makes the world a better place		
Allows me to exercise my creativity, freedom of expression, and imagination		
Requires or permits travel		
Is predictable, concise, and measured		
Has long-term job stability and a steady income		
Has high-earning opportunities to live a robust lifestyle		

Conversation Questions

- What was your very first job (i.e., way of earning cash) growing up?
- What jobs did you have in the past that were not good fits? How did they help guide you to where you are now?
- What jobs were good fits? How did you use them as stepping stones to arrive at this point in your life?
- How does unpaid labor (e.g., cooking, cleaning, parenting, household management, volunteering) inform your larger understanding of work?
- If your current work doesn't fulfill your sense of purpose, what do you imagine such work would entail?
- If we weren't married, would you change your occupation?
- What volunteer activity do you find joy in, or what do you think you would find joy in?
- Do you have any biases around gender and work?

Ritual of Connection

Get two pieces of scrap paper, one for each of you. Now consider this question: "If wage and familial responsibilities weren't factors, what kind of a job would bring my partner the most joy and satisfaction, and why?" Spend a few minutes writing down your best guesses and then trade papers. Discuss how close or how far off your answers are.

Goals, Passions & Aspirations

This section invites you to identify and share your most potent aspirations. What do you yearn for, and what goals propel you forward? By openly discussing these dimensions of your inner world, you'll unlock one of the essential patterns found in satisfied couples: supporting each other's dreams.

So this isn't about planning for the future; it's about dreaming together in the present—how you wish to live out your life as a person and as a couple and how to live without regrets. This requires vulnerability and a bit of imagination.

Exercise

1. Dream with your partner about what lies ahead. Think about experiences you hope to have, accomplishments you hope to achieve, places you wish to see, people you wish to meet, and life changes you hope to make before you "kick the bucket." Don't limit your dreaming—think big and bold without holding back—and cheerlead your partner to do the same. Remember, dreaming is different from doing, but it's also a prerequisite for it.

2. Write down your dreams of all sizes—everything from cleaning out your storage area to a yearlong trip around the globe. Circle any dreams you would regret not fulfilling. After you've both done this exercise, share one of your big dreams and one of your small dreams with each other. Support each other in taking steps toward those dreams *now*.

PARTNER A'S BUCKET LIST

1. ______________________________
2. ______________________________
3. ______________________________
4. ______________________________
5. ______________________________
6. ______________________________
7. ______________________________
8. ______________________________
9. ______________________________
10. ______________________________

PARTNER B'S BUCKET LIST

1. ______________________________
2. ______________________________
3. ______________________________
4. ______________________________
5. ______________________________
6. ______________________________
7. ______________________________
8. ______________________________
9. ______________________________
10. ______________________________

Conversation Questions

* What surprised you most about my bucket list?
* How can I support you in achieving one of your big dreams in the coming weeks, months, and years?
* How can I support you in achieving one of your small dreams in the next couple of days?
* Which of your dreams do you think will be the most difficult to achieve, and what are the potential roadblocks?
* What fears do you have around being unable to achieve one or more of your dreams?
* What is a dream you had in the past that became a reality?
* What is one step we can take this week to move closer to fulfilling a shared dream?

Ritual of Connection

Look around your home and see if there are any "trophies" you've collected by achieving past goals. It could be an actual trophy or evidence of a completed DIY project (e.g., a photograph). Share the stories of those triumphs and congratulate each other on a job well done!

What Makes Me Feel Loved?

In *The 5 Love Languages*, Gary Chapman categorizes the way people tend to give and receive love. Issues often arise when a couple doesn't know each other's love language, as this can result in unmet needs or resentment around unrecognized efforts.

Understanding and learning to speak each other's love language contributes to the richness of your connection by helping you build a shared vocabulary. Additionally, you'll learn how to be a more responsive lover. This section invites you to share the intricacies of these principles.

Exercise

Partnering with another human is a commitment to meeting them where they are and attempting (as best you can) to meet their needs. Read the descriptions of the love languages and each of you select your primary and secondary love language. Note whether the ways you prefer to give love are the same or different from the ways you prefer to receive it.

Quality Time: You most adore being together with the person or people you love. A special occasion may be best spent with your partner or an intimate group of your favorite people. A perfect evening may not involve a specific activity, as long as you get to be present with your tribe or person. Limiting distractions and boosting undivided attention resonates with your love song.

Words of Affirmation: You light up when your partner compliments you, verbally acknowledges your hard work, or simply uses words to affirm their love and devotion. A phrase we love is "I could live off a salary of your compliments."

Gifts: A small token that someone was thinking about you or found something that represented your interests fills your cup. An elaborate gift of generosity can also hit the spot when tied with just how much this person adores you.

Physical Touch: Physical touch is soothing, loving, and welcome. A hug, snuggle, hand squeeze, and back scratch can go a long way in helping you feel loved.

Acts of Service: When a loved one goes out of their way to focus on your needs and offers to help, it makes you feel loved and important to that person. A handmade cappuccino delivered in bed or folding of your laundry can make you feel connected and adored.

Conversation Questions

- Which specific actions or expressions make you feel most loved and cherished?
- Does it feel natural or unnatural for you to speak my love language?
- How does open and honest communication contribute to your feeling loved?
- How do sincere apologies and forgiveness contribute to your feeling loved?
- How can we create a safe space for each other to express our needs and desires?
- When you try to show me love, do you feel that I recognize it? If not, what would you like me to be on the lookout for?
- What shared activities or experiences make us feel deeply connected?
- How can we re-create or build upon past experiences or shared moments when we both felt exceptionally loved?
- How can we better show each other gratitude for our efforts to show love?

Ritual of Connection

Take turns checking in with your partner to see what would make them feel loved. See if you can create a daily ritual of asking for specific guidance. For example, Laura has a daily ritual of asking her partner each morning, "How can I make you feel loved today?" She does this to eliminate guesswork and ensure that she can meet her husband at his point of need.

Perceptions around Money & Time

If you want to know where your priorities lie, look at how you spend your time and money. These limited resources—along with others like physical space and energy—say a lot about how we assign meaning in the world. Time and money are especially complicated because they dictate so many of our lifestyle choices. Here you'll explore the ways your individual perspectives on time and money contribute to the landscape of your shared life.

This section invites you to consider your perceptions around these resources, but it isn't a conversation about practicalities. It's a thoughtful consideration of how your individual perspectives weave together.

Exercise

Money means different things to different people, but two prominent meanings are security and freedom. When partners disagree here (i.e., to one partner saving equals security, and to another spending equals freedom), there's often a visceral reaction to protect your security and/or freedom from being compromised by your partner. This is why many people believe that money is often at the root of marital dissolution.

1. Aside from security or freedom, there are dozens of additional meanings that money could represent. In the space provided, brainstorm as many more meanings for money as you can think of. Include security and freedom as well. These meanings don't have to resonate with you personally. Simply see how many you can come up with together in a couple of minutes.

2. When you've exhausted ideas, take turns circling the two or three that resonate most with you. Discuss your choices and see what you can learn from each other without focusing on the mathematics of money.

Conversation Questions

- How do you feel about the way we are using our time and money?
- Do you have any ideas about how we can be more effective or efficient with our time and money?
- What is your general philosophy around time, and how do your behaviors reflect this belief?
- What is your general philosophy around money, and how do your behaviors reflect this belief?
- What are our similarities and differences around the concept of time?
- What are our similarities and differences around the concept of money?
- How do we organize our shared life when it comes to time (day to day, hour to hour, week to week, month to month, year to year)?
- What do you feel we are "getting right" in terms of how we spend our time and money?
- What decisions can we make today that would bring us closer and help us feel more confident in how we spend our time and money?

Ritual of Connection

Brainstorm all the things you can measure in your life (e.g., money, time, the size of your home, the length of your commute). Now imagine if any of those things grew by 20 percent overnight. How would life be different? And what if they shrank by 20 percent? As you play with this, pay attention to what it reveals for each of you about what you value.

Current Values

Few people can clearly define their ethical or moral code. For many, these codes are rooted in religious, societal, or familial belief systems. For others, it's more intrinsic, flowing out of a fundamental sense of right and wrong. Regardless, it's important to understand how your internal code has served as a compass to guide your personal and shared journey.

This section invites you to explore how you navigate the complexities of right and wrong—and how the context of time, place, and culture plays a role. By openly discussing these dimensions, you'll more clearly define for each other and yourselves the basis for your choices and commitments.

Exercise

Review the following list together, and with different-colored pens to keep track of your choices, circle the top-10 core values you most identify with. These may be qualities you most value in other people or in yourself as well as qualities you aspire to embody.

Accountability
Achievement
Adaptability
Adventurousness
Altruism
Ambition
Artistry
Authenticity
Balance
Beauty
Being the best
Belonging
Career
Caring
Collaboration
Commitment
Community
Compassion
Competence
Confidence
Connection
Contentment
Contribution
Cooperation
Courage
Creativity
Determination
Dignity
Diversity
Efficiency
Empathy
Entrepreneurism
Environment
Equality
Ethics
Excellence
Experience
Fairness
Faith
Family
Financial stability
Forgiveness
Freedom
Friendship
Fun
Future generations
Generosity
Grace
Gratitude
Growth
Harmony
Health
Honesty
Honor
Hope
Humility
Humor
Inclusion
Independence
Ingenuity
Initiative
Integrity
Intuition
Joy
Justice
Kindness
Knowledge
Leadership
Learning
Legacy
Leisure
Love
Loyalty
Making a difference
Nature
Openness
Optimism
Order
Passion
Patience
Patriotism
Peace
Perseverance
Positivity
Power
Pride
Productivity
Recognition
Reliability
Resourcefulness
Respect
Responsibility
Risk-taking
Sacrifice
Safety
Security
Self-discipline
Self-expression
Serenity
Service
Simplicity
Solitude
Spirituality
Sportsmanship
Stewardship
Strength
Success
Teamwork
Thoughtfulness
Thrift
Time
Tradition
Travel
Trustworthiness
Truth
Understanding
Uniqueness
Usefulness
Vision
Vulnerability
Wealth
Well-being
Wholeheartedness
Wisdom

Conversation Questions

* Which of your values were instilled in you from childhood?
* Which of your values do you think you inherited from your religious/spiritual tradition?
* Which values are we most aligned on?
* Do you appreciate or respect certain values in other people that you wish you could embody, and what might be stopping you from embodying those values?
* In what situation have you compromised your values, and what was the outcome and lesson?
* Do our friends and family generally seem aligned with our values? Why or why not?
* What specific things can we do in the next 30, 60, or 90 days to reinforce some of the values we hold dear?

Ritual of Connection

Recall your earliest memory of a moral conflict and share the details with your partner. Maybe you chose to do something you knew was wrong and eventually confessed. Perhaps you witnessed something you felt was wrong but kept it a secret. The stickier and more nuanced, the more fruitful this exercise, so don't hold back. Why do you think you still remember this moment?

Fears & Phobias

The monster under the bed loses its power when you turn on the light. We all have "monsters" that haunt us from time to time. What fears and phobias lurk in the corners of your mind? Shining a light on these fears is a critical step in navigating the path to freedom.

This section invites you to discuss your fears and phobias to create a space for personal safety, mutual understanding, and emotional support as you negotiate with the monsters under your shared bed. This is also an opportunity to differentiate between rational fears and intrusive fears that don't serve you or your relationship.

Exercise

Being present for our partner's pain can be one of the most difficult relational tasks to endure, especially when we have no way of solving the problem or are working through something ourselves. It turns out that one of the most healing things you can do for both you and your partner is to provide a safe space for them to vent their stress, fear, and pain without solving the problem or casting judgment.

Follow these steps, which are based on Drs. Gottmans' stress-reducing conversation guidelines, to create a road map for discussing stress, fears, and pain outside the relationship.

A. Set a timer for 10 minutes.

B. The speaker gets the floor to unload any fears, anxieties, stress, and worries that concern them. The topic of concern can be anything outside the relationship. It can be difficult to be the listener and the topic of conversation, so for this conversation, the speaker leaves the listener out of the vent session.

C. The listener's role is to NOT try to solve the problem or offer any advice. The primary job as the listener is to show genuine concern, empathy, and validation for the speaker's pain. As the listener, maintain eye contact, nod and smile, and give verbal affirmation cues to encourage safety. Reflect back empathic statements like "That does sound like a lot" and "Of course you worry about that."

D. When the timer sounds, reset it and switch roles as speaker and listener.

Conversation Questions

- How would you define "anxiety"?
- When you were growing up, how did your parents/caregivers handle their fears, anxieties, stress, and worries?
- What role do fears, anxieties, stress, and worries play in your life?
- Have you experienced heightened periods of anxiety, and if so, what was going on?
- What is your relationship to fear, and how has it evolved over the course of your life?
- Has anxiety played a role in your experience of our relationship?
- What tools do you use to manage your anxiety?
- How can I best support you when you are feeling scared or anxious?

Ritual of Connection

The 5-4-3-2-1 method is a quick grounding tool when you're feeling anxious or need to redirect your thoughts to the present moment to calm yourself. Practice this skill together by following these steps: (1) Look for five things you can see, (2) Focus on four things you can touch, (3) Listen for three things you can hear, (4) Find two things you can smell, and (5) Identify one thing you can taste.

Lessons Learned

Each of us collects unexpected wisdom in our journey toward maturity; some lessons are harder than others and may have more of an impact on us. What lessons have reshaped your perspectives, and how do they influence your present selves? How do your surprise lessons weave together? How do they show up in your daily life?

This section invites you to share the unexpected insights you've each gained over the years. Discussing your acquired wisdom is more than a dialogue about personal growth; it's a reminder of your own resilience and an opportunity to see this same strength and perseverance in your partner.

Exercise

SUPPLIES: stationery and pens

1. In this exercise you'll each write a love letter of appreciation to someone who's worthy of praise and is near and dear to you—yourselves! Find a peaceful setting and a firm writing surface, and take along a yummy beverage to enjoy during this process. Set a timer for 15 minutes. Begin your letters with the phrase "Remember when . . ."
2. In this letter, highlight the strong, wise, seasoned version of you who is here today. Feel free to visit distinct memories of growth, which are often punctuated with hardship and pain, and how you persevered. Finish your letter by noting some of your favorite attributes, brilliant character flaws, charming habits, and lovely quirks.
3. Take turns reading your letters aloud to each other.

Conversation Questions

- What subtle lessons from your life quietly but clearly shape how you show up in relationships today?
- If our relationship were a film, what recent plot twist would make audiences delight in the surprise?
- What missteps have turned out to be unexpected masterpieces in your life, and what's their role in our current story?
- How have your journeys (literal and metaphorical) provided unexpected small lessons that have come to symbolize your growth and maturity?
- Reflecting on unexpected moments and surprises, what lessons have you stumbled upon that now shape your thinking?
- Considering our journey together, what surprising lessons have we learned about each other along the way? How have these informed our present connection?
- Which major life transitions have we gone through that have contributed to our present sense of ourselves as a couple?

Ritual of Connection

Stand face-to-face and take each other in, looking without judgment. What can you get curious about? What can you see that you haven't noticed before? What can you learn about your partner just by observing their posture, skin, eyes, and energy? Mentally embrace the wise being who stands before you with love and appreciation.

Sexual Interests & Explorations

Perhaps more than any other topic, sex is loaded with unspoken and unexplored assumptions about what should and shouldn't be. This varies from person to person based on their life experiences, but it remains a delicate topic.

Sex was a taboo topic in Zach's home growing up. It wasn't that it was off-limits as much as they simply didn't talk about it. He only started to fully understand the complexities of sex once he began working it out as an adult, primarily through conversation.

This section invites you to share the intricacies of your sexuality to increase connection. You'll consider fantasies that ignite your desires as well as anxieties that impact your intimacy. Even more than in previous conversations, you'll want to create a safe space for mutual understanding and shared vulnerability. Commit to being tender and caring as you consider the factors that shape the intimate dimensions of your relationship.

Exercise

1. Giving and receiving mutual pleasure requires clear and direct communication. For this exercise, partners will take turns giving and receiving a 15-minute massage. This helps each of you practice giving your partner instructions to maximize your pleasure and helps you learn how to listen to your partner's guidance.

2. The purpose of this massage is to maximize Partner B's pleasure, but only according to what Partner B dictates as pleasurable. Partner B begins by giving direct instructions as to location, texture, and pressure to begin massaging (e.g., start massaging my head with medium pressure, using your fingertips in a circular pattern).

3. Partner A will do this until otherwise instructed, as Partner A cannot do anything else unless specifically instructed by Partner B. So if Partner B becomes bored of a location or wants a different texture or pressure, they must verbally instruct Partner A to do so. Continue this way for 15 minutes, then switch roles.

Conversation Questions

- What were some of your formative lessons about sex, and how have they shaped your current view of intimacy?
- How has your understanding of sexual health and wellness evolved over time?
- How do you define "sexual intimacy"?
- In what ways are our definitions of "sexual intimacy" similar, and how do they differ?
- Has your sexual desire changed over time, and if so, why do you think that is?
- How have cultural influences (media, society, or family) impacted your perceptions of sexuality?
- What turns you on and what turns you off sexually?
- How can we cocreate an environment where we feel comfortable exploring previously unspoken sexual fantasies together?
- How can we embrace our sensuality and infuse more passion into our intimate moments?
- Do laughter and playfulness contribute to a more joyful and relaxed sexual atmosphere between us?

Ritual of Connection

Together, redesign the purpose of your bedroom to support sleep and intimate connection. What items need to be cleared out to create space? What kind of lighting invites softness and intimacy? Does your bedding need a refresh? Do you need a lock on the door for privacy? If you're unable to make changes right now, jot down 5 to 10 ways you can adapt your bedroom to create a space you can both relax and play in intimately.

CHAPTER 6

Returning to Each Other

In this chapter you'll look at your daily life as a couple to tease out the simple joys of your connection. As always, approach this topic with curiosity and compassion. It's not about fixing what's broken; it's about creating something new. Listen to each other's desires for the marriage. Think of it as a shared art project where you paint the canvas together.

This is your opportunity to become more rooted in the current principles and practices that resonate with both of you today. So grab a cup of coffee or tea or whatever gets your conversational juices flowing and learn what you can about the love, connection, and joy you both deserve.

Favorite Parts of the Marriage

In this section you'll explore the parts of your marriage that bring you joy. Picture this conversation as a cinematic reel of your love story. What scenes do you replay? These cherished moments are the pulse of your relationship.

By exploring your favorite parts, you're unlocking the secrets to a more connected present. In fact, keep *the present* in mind as you reflect on these stories. Get ready to shine a light on the extraordinary moments that define your union. And keep an eye on how these things enhance your bond in the here and now. Let the conversation unveil the treasures that add vibrancy to your shared narrative.

Exercise

1. In this exercise, you'll take turns tapping into the part of your memory that replays sounds that contributed to the joy of your life together.

   Close your eyes and recall moments of love, connection, joy, peace, and belonging. Once you have a specific scene in your mind, tap into the sounds that were present at that moment (e.g., laughter, rain, music, boat motor, waves, wind, excited shouts, the pitter-patter of feet, soothing voices, birds chirping, merry-go-round). Share the soundtrack of your love story with your partner, moment by moment, as you replay this scene.

2. When done, take a moment to bring those feelings into the present moment, focusing on gratitude and joy as you connect with each other today.

Conversation Questions

- What are some memories from our marriage that bring joy to your heart?
- What milestones in our shared journey are you most happy about?
- What are the qualities of our relationship that you admire the most?
- What are your favorite ways to show love and appreciation?
- Which types of activities or experiences do you value most during our quality time together?
- What are some moments of laughter and joy that brought us closer?
- What aspects of our physical and emotional connection do you find most fulfilling and enjoyable?
- Which aspects of our communication style do you appreciate the most?
- What are some things about our marriage that you feel grateful for?
- Which spontaneous moments do you treasure the most?

Ritual of Connection

Close your eyes and bring your attention to your breath. Focus specifically on the rise and fall of your chest for several minutes. Now shift your attention from inside to outside by listening to your surroundings for a few minutes more. What do you hear? How many sounds can you identify? Zero in on one specific sound at a time. Afterward, share with each other what you heard and what the experience of listening was like for you.

What Family Means to Us

For most couples, the definition of "family" changes throughout the years. This section invites you to explore new roles or dimensions that have shaped your current family life. Exploring this topic helps you identify common ground and potential areas of divergence, paving the way for compromise and collaboration in the future.

Delving into the concept of family—whether it's a family of two or more and perhaps includes four-leggeds—strengthens emotional intimacy, as partners share vulnerable aspects of their pasts and articulate their desires for the future. Let the conversations unfold naturally, and give yourselves permission to learn something new as you refine your definition of "family" together.

Exercise

SUPPLIES: colored pencils or crayons

In this activity you'll be working together to design a coat of arms, a visual representation of your family (using symbols, colors, and a motto), traditionally overlaid on a shield. Historically, a coat of arms was used in battles and tournaments to tell who was on which side. Your shared coat of arms reinforces that you're both on the same side in your family.

Work as a team to select a symbol or grouping of symbols that are meaningful to your family, and draw them in the shield, then brainstorm a family motto that clearly expresses your shared values and purpose, and write it in the ribbon below the shield.

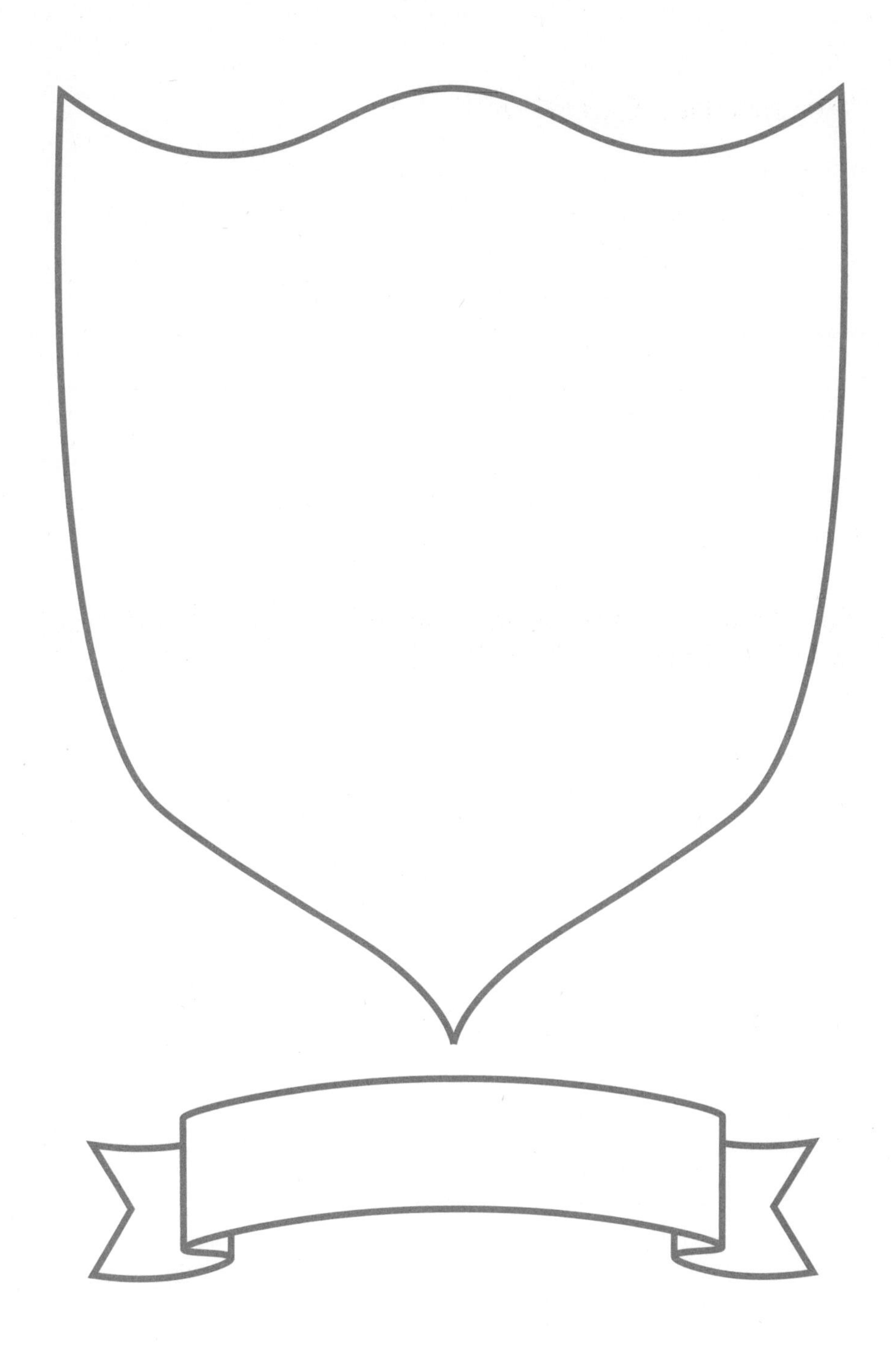

Conversation Questions

* How do we express love for one another in our family?
* What ideas do you have about responsibility, accountability, and discipline, and how do you think they should apply in our home?
* What traditions are important to us to celebrate in our home?
* In our family, what do we consider sacred?
* When our family is at its happiest, what are we usually doing?
* What do we find meaning in doing as part of our family life?
* What word or phrase do you find yourself repeating a lot in our home?
* How do we most like to spend time together as a family?
* What is something you wish others would say about our family?

Ritual of Connection

Bring to mind a couple who knows you well. How do you each think these friends would describe your family? When telling others about you, is there anything specific you'd like them to include or leave out? Note any places where you may not be aligned about how you think others perceive you.

In Lockstep

Turn your attention to the rhythms of your shared responsibilities and finding the perfect harmony. Imagine it as fine-tuning the engine of your partnership. How do you each approach tasks, and how can these approaches complement each other?

As you explore this topic, ask yourselves: What unique skills and perspectives do we each bring to the table as we try to solve our shared problems? By syncing up about task orientations, you're not just managing to-do lists; you're cocreating a context for collaboration.

Exercise

1. Earlier, in the exercise on page 106, you identified your roles and responsibilities in your marriage. Now it's time to identify and ritualize a system that allows you to easily communicate about the comings and goings of your busy lives. There are countless ways to structure your communication. Here are two suggestions to keep you organized:

   A. In a common area, keep a whiteboard with a calendar feature, a shopping list, and important to-dos for each one of you.

   B. Communicate through a digital calendar or project-management software such as Trello or Cozi.

2. Once you've chosen a system for sharing information, the next step is to establish regular weekly check-ins for verbally touching base and clarifying expectations. Make note of your agreement here:

   When and where will we meet weekly? ______________________

   How long will this meeting last? ______________________

   Who will be in attendance (e.g., the entire family, additional caretakers, just us)? ______________________

   ____

3. Use this structure for your meeting or come up with your own:

   A. **Gratitude:** Start the meeting with gratitude for each other or someone else in your family for something specific that occurred this week.

   B. **Schedule:** Discuss events coming up this week. Is there anything out of the ordinary or that needs to be discussed in further detail?

   C. **Chores:** Discuss distribution of chores and to-do items. What specific department needs attention this week? (e.g., If you are hosting a dinner party, is there any special attention that needs to be paid to housecleaning or grocery shopping?)

   D. **Goals and accomplishments:** What goals do you have for the week? What support do you need? What accomplishments can you celebrate from last week?

Conversation Questions

* What are your natural strengths regarding household management?
* What tasks around the house do you find most draining?
* What simple joys and pleasures do you derive from taking care of our home?
* Which of your responsibilities would you like to trade or outsource?
* Which of my responsibilities would you like to try your hand at?
* How can we make certain household responsibilities more fun and enjoyable?
* What chores need to be refined or adapted to our current needs?
* Which chores can we do together to make them go more quickly?
* Are we meeting each other's expectations around the home, and if not, what can we each do to clarify or compromise?

Ritual of Connection

Express gratitude to your partner for three skills that contribute to the function of your household and shared responsibilities. Is your partner an amazing cook? Do you appreciate the time and energy they put into organizing the home? What do you do that complements the roles your partner handles? Share your appreciation for each other.

Experiencing Loss & Illness

In the ebb and flow of life, there are moments of loss and loneliness that require us to grapple with themes of grief. This section invites you to sit together, share stories of heartache, and explore the nuances of sadness.

Why embark on this conversation? Think of it as creating a space for shared compassion. Delving into this topic, you can explore the synergies found in the face of grief and how to better support each other during these vulnerable moments. Let the conversation be a compassionate duet, fostering closeness and connection amid life's complexities.

Exercise

1. Some grief rituals are bound to our spiritual beliefs, culture, or family of origin. Funerals are the most obvious, but there are others. For example, Laura found a sealed mason jar on the beach with a note written inside of it. The evening before, she'd noticed a group of friends gathered on the beach, surrounded by candles, watching the sunset. The note revealed that the group had been grieving and honoring a recently deceased friend by writing letters to him and tossing them into the ocean.

2. Some people might watch their departed loved one's favorite movie; others might visit the cemetery; some might write their loved one a letter, as that group of friends did; and the list goes on. What rituals of grief honor loss in your family? Jot them down here:

Conversation Questions

- What rituals of loss did you experience when you were growing up (e.g., funerals, memorials, religious grieving periods)?
- Which rituals make sense to you and which don't?
- Whom have you grieved for due to the loss of a relationship and/or death?
- How do you usually cope with grief?
- What other aspects of your life have you grieved (e.g., loss of job, health, identity, pet)?
- In what ways have we supported each other during the grieving process?
- What advice would you give to someone who is grieving?
- How does it feel to be vulnerable when you are grieving?
- When have we needed to rely on our resilience as a couple when facing a shared loss?

Ritual of Connection

Find a memento, photograph, or heirloom that holds special meaning to you of someone you have lost, either physically or emotionally. Take turns sharing the stories behind your items and the evolution of your feelings as you experienced the loss of this relationship.

Getting Older

The path through life takes us through phases that sometimes sneak up on us. Midlife is one of those phases. Whether or not you're presently in this phase, this section invites you to delve into the themes of aging. Think of it as crafting a road map for the next chapter of your adventure.

Understanding how you each approach the idea of aging can bring you closer. What aspirations do you share for the older versions of yourselves? How can you best support each other along the way? Let these conversations be a celebration of the years you've shared, the ones you currently share, and the ones around the corner.

Exercise

Look at the "wheel of life" (there's one for each of you). Each has eight sections representing a different area of life: fun, health, money, friends, partner, physical health, emotional health, and personal growth. For each area, jot down words that represent your aspirations for yourself as you age. When done, share your wheel with your partner. Notice your similarities and differences.

PARTNER A

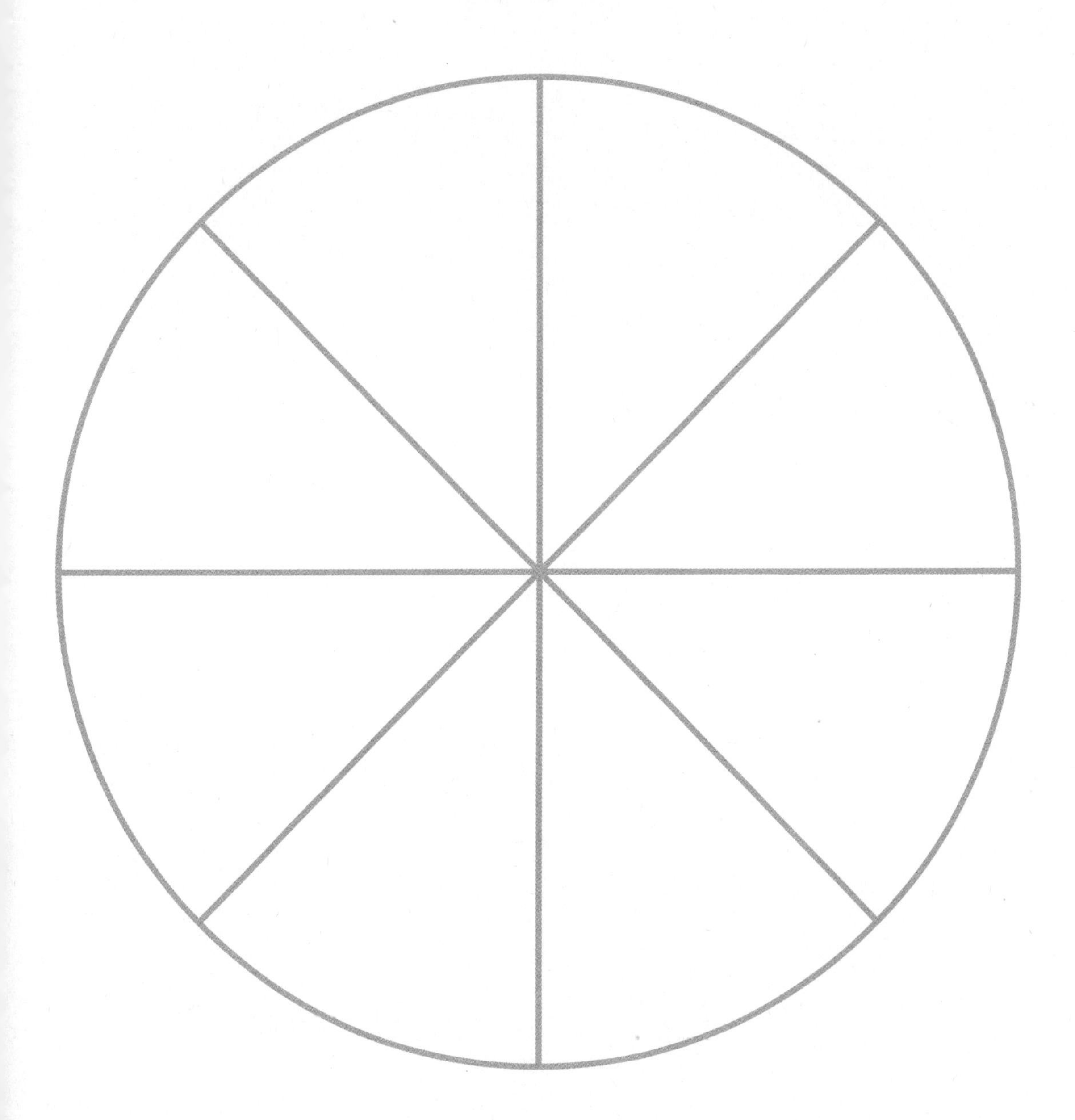

PARTNER B

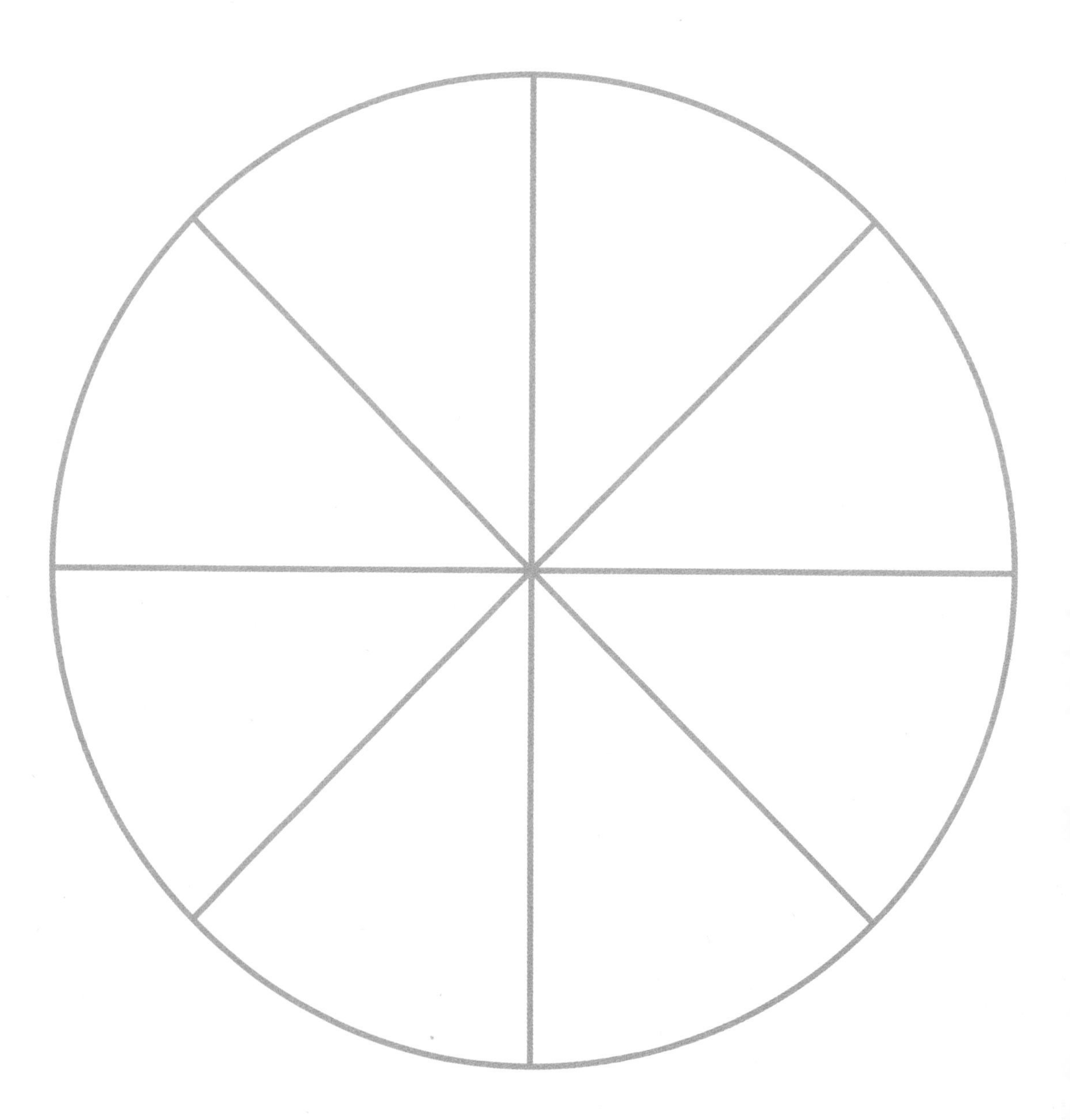

Conversation Questions

- How do you feel about getting older?
- Are you grasping for youth or embracing the aging process, or are you somewhere in the middle?
- What does it mean to you to “age gracefully”?
- What would you say is the most rewarding part of getting older?
- What is your biggest fear about aging?
- What wisdom do you have now that you didn’t have in your youth?
- What older couple do we admire, and why?
- What older couple do we *not* want to be like, and why?
- What do we like to do now that we didn’t enjoy when we first got together?
- How can we best support each other now so that we can each realize our aspirations when we’re older?

Ritual of Connection

Has anyone ever told you that you are “youthful” or “have an old soul,” regardless of your biological age or maybe even how your body feels? Share with each other what age you identify as and discuss why you feel that way. Take turns telling stories of when you first began to identify with that age.

Coming Together in Times of Stress

We all have coping strategies that anchor us during turbulent times. In this section you'll take a closer look at how you each handle stress and how understanding these strategies can strengthen your bond. Embracing this topic gives you the opportunity to assess the gifts and perspectives you each bring when the seas get rough. You'll learn how to ensure that you keep heading in the same direction.

You are more resilient and equipped than you might imagine. As you explore the coping strategies that anchor your connection, consider it a grand adventure. Seize this as an opportunity to celebrate the joy of mutual support.

Exercise

Coping skills are the emotional tools we use when we hit rough patches and experience stress. Not all coping skills are created equal, and there's no one-size-fits-all approach. Some coping skills can give you temporary relief from your pain and make you feel better (see the examples in this worksheet), while others have unintended consequences.

Review the worksheet, and for each coping skill jot down what you have done that may have helped in the past. Also make note of any new ideas you'd like to try. Some of these coping skills are solo activities, while others rely on the strength of the relationship to bring you back to a space of safety and comfort.

COPING SKILL	DEFINITION	PARTNER A	PARTNER B
Distraction	Absorb your mind into something (e.g., conversation, listening to a podcast, reading).		
Grounding	Get out of your head and into your body or the world (e.g., walking on grass barefoot, yoga, exercise).		
Emotional release	Let it all out (e.g., a good hard cry, screaming).		
Self-love	Treat yourself extra special and gently (e.g., hot bath, massage, a special meal).		
Thought challenge	Be critical of your thoughts and identify how your distressing or unkind thoughts may be untrue (e.g., "I am not lovable is not true because my mother calls me every Sunday to check in").		

COPING SKILL	DEFINITION	PARTNER A	PARTNER B
Access your higher self	Give unselfishly to others who would benefit (e.g., volunteer at a dog shelter, smile at passersby).		
Rally your resources	Look beyond yourself for support (e.g., call a handy friend or family member who can help you mend your fence).		
Stay on the same team	Lock arms and remember that your partner is not your enemy but your teammate (e.g., take your partner's hand in the fight and let them know they aren't alone).		
Practice tolerance	Remember that stress is short term (e.g., extend grace when you recognize your partner is also struggling).		
Gratitude	Look around you to find the parts of your world you appreciate (e.g., keep a daily journal of appreciations).		

Conversation Questions

- What coping skill do you find most effective in making you feel better?
- Which unhelpful or consequential coping skills would you like to replace?
- What type of coping skills did you observe in your family of origin growing up, and how do you think that impacts your tool kit today?
- How can we best support each other when one of us is struggling (e.g., remind the other to use their coping skills)?
- When faced with a stressful scenario, what coping skills did we use as a couple to manage stress successfully?
- What additional resources might we need to be able to weather a season of hardship?
- What is one of my natural gifts or skills you can rely on in difficult times?

Ritual of Connection

Discuss the most recent time each of you experienced feelings of hopelessness or helplessness. It's human nature to try to relieve ourselves of distressing thoughts and feelings by reaching for anything that makes us feel better. What coping skill did you use to make yourself feel better in the wake of this recent distressing event? Take turns sharing more about the coping skill you used. What worked? What didn't? Were there unintended consequences?

Physical Intimacy & Romance

Are you ready for a deep, connection-building conversation about a vital aspect of your connection: physical intimacy, romance, and sex? As you unravel this topic, you'll take a closer look at what sparks joy and fulfillment in your romantic life and how to enhance this aspect of your marriage.

Sex can be a touchy subject, especially if it's mixed up with shame, but your marriage can be the safest place to explore it. By discussing sexual intimacy and romance, you're not only addressing desires but also sculpting a shared narrative of pleasure, safety, and closeness. Tap into your compassion and curiosity, and try to have fun!

Exercise

Unabashed intimacy begins with good, open conversation, and the Yes-No-Maybe game is a great conversation starter to explore what each of you finds erotic, pleasurable, and enjoyable. The best time to talk about sex is *not* while you are having sex but before you begin, so complete this exercise outside the bedroom.

Review the checklist (there's one for each of you), and then fill out the checklists independently by checking the box for "yes" ("Yes, I think I would try that"), "no" ("No, I don't think I would like that"), or "maybe" ("Maybe I would give that a try") for each item on the list. Complete the checklists before diving into the conversation questions.

PARTNER A

	YES	NO	MAYBE
Biting			
Blindfolds			
Caressing			
Dancing for partner			
Dominance/submission			
Exhibitionism			
Finger sucking			
Foot kissing			
Giving oral sex			
Hair pulling			
Ice play			
Journaling about sex			
Lap dances from/for partner			
Making videos			
Massage			
Masturbating in front of partner			
Nibbling ears and neck			
Outdoor sex			
Play with anus			

PARTNER A

	YES	NO	MAYBE
Playing with sex toys			
Reading erotica			
Receiving oral sex			
Restricting your partner's movement			
Role-playing			
Scratching			
Sex in the shower			
Sex with lights on			
Sexting			
Sharing fantasies			
Sharing my sexual history			
Shaving your partner's body			
Striptease for partner			
Talking dirty			
Using a gag			
Using food items in sex play			
Using lubricant			
Using oils and lotions			

PARTNER B

	YES	NO	MAYBE
Biting			
Blindfolds			
Caressing			
Dancing for partner			
Dominance/submission			
Exhibitionism			
Finger sucking			
Foot kissing			
Giving oral sex			
Hair pulling			
Ice play			
Journaling about sex			
Lap dances from/for partner			
Making videos			
Massage			
Masturbating in front of partner			
Nibbling ears and neck			
Outdoor sex			
Play with anus			

PARTNER B

	YES	NO	MAYBE
Playing with sex toys			
Reading erotica			
Receiving oral sex			
Restricting your partner's movement			
Role-playing			
Scratching			
Sex in the shower			
Sex with lights on			
Sexting			
Sharing fantasies			
Sharing my sexual history			
Shaving your partner's body			
Striptease for partner			
Talking dirty			
Using a gag			
Using food items in sex play			
Using lubricant			
Using oils and lotions			

Conversation Questions

- What are we both interested in trying?
- What were you pleasantly surprised to see on my list of what I would be willing to try?
- What were your reasons for choosing "maybe" for each of the activities you selected in that category?
- What were your reasons for choosing "no" for each of the activities you selected in that category?
- How can we make one of the mutual "yes" activities special, safe, and pleasurable for both of us?
- Have your erotic interests changed over time and, if so, in what way?
- What is your favorite way to be approached for sex? Which sexual advances do you prefer?
- Would you rather initiate intimacy or be invited?
- How can I let you know with compassion if I don't want to be sexually intimate?
- What makes each of us most comfortable during erotic encounters?

Ritual of Connection

Recall one of the hottest, steamiest, most sexually pleasurable experiences you've shared with each other. It may have been years ago, early in your relationship-building phase, or it may have been last night, ripe with all your sexual wisdom and confidence. Share your memories with each other, going into as much sensory detail as you can, and describe why that experience made your all-time-delight list.

Rules & Relational Identities

You've just arrived at a discussion of a pivotal aspect of your shared life: rules that govern your daily lives (spoken and unspoken) and your relational identities (i.e., your identity in the relationship). How each of you defines your relational identity directs most of how you move through your daily lives and the rules you follow.

As you embark on this topic, focus on learning how to ensure your shared life cultivates closeness. Let your conversations be a creative exercise in forming a unique relational game that brings edification to you both. Your goal is to purposely create the rules of the game so you can both enjoy it.

Exercise

Review the following list of popular relationship "rules." You may notice that some of these blanket statements don't resonate with your relationship, while others do. Decide together whether any of these rules have a place in your relationship. Don't get hung up on semantics; focus on the spirit of the rule. Once you have a sense of these rules, brainstorm together 10 of your own agreed-upon rules in the space provided.

A. Assume your partner's intent and don't question otherwise.

B. Do not threaten to quit, divorce, or leave the relationship.

C. Don't speak poorly of your partner behind their back.

D. Don't compare your relationship to others; nothing is as it seems on the outside anyway.

E. It is better to be heard and understood than to be right.

F. Don't stray from our sexual agreement (i.e., monogamy or otherwise).

G. When your partner asks for space, give it.

H. Support your partner in their relationships outside of the relationship.

I. Maintain privacy around personal and relational issues.

J. Repair, apologize, and acknowledge early and often.

K. Love your partner unconditionally.

L. Be your partner's best friend.

M. Conflict is a healthy part of relationships.

N. Be your partner's ally and teammate through hard times.

O. Understand that your partner is different and also wonderful even when not just like you.

THE RULES OF OUR RELATIONSHIP

1. ______________________________
   ____
2. ______________________________
   ____
3. ______________________________
   ____
4. ______________________________
   ____
5. ______________________________
   ____
6. ______________________________
   ____
7. ______________________________
   ____
8. ______________________________
   ____
9. ______________________________
   ____
10. ______________________________
    ____

Conversation Questions

- How do you feel about the word "rules" when it comes to exploring our marriage? Is there another word we prefer to use in its place?
- Which of the sample rules didn't resonate with you, and why?
- Which rules do we live by that you think are outdated or no longer apply to our relationship?
- Would you consider our identity as a couple traditional, conventional, or transitional?
- How do our relational identities complement each other?
- Do we fundamentally disagree on any of the rules? Taking one rule at a time, how can we reach an understanding?
- When did we have an expectation of each other that felt like a violation of our rules?
- How often should we need to revisit the rules of our relationship?
- What would be a good ritual to create to evaluate our explicit agreements?

Ritual of Connection

Have you ever seen a comedy where people switch bodies and live as each other for a time? What do you think it would be like to switch places with each other? Talk about what you think a day in the life of your partner would be like. Describe the elements you would and wouldn't enjoy. What do you think it would be like to be married to you?

Rituals & Routines

Rituals and routines help us measure time and create meaning. They are the heartbeat of a relationship. Here you'll explore the way your current routines contribute to your relational melody and how enhancing these rituals can deepen your connection.

While you've been exploring rituals of connection throughout this workbook, take a closer look at the existing rituals (or ones you'd like to implement) on a more regular basis. By discussing rituals, you're affirming your commitment to an intentional relationship and composing a shared legacy of togetherness and purpose. You'll examine the sweet, simple moments you can elevate to create a harmonious daily cadence.

Exercise

Have you ever spent time around couples who have lived and loved one another for a very long time? Their habits of the heart are beautifully entwined throughout their daily lives, weaving in and out of everyday moments as reminders of love and connection. For example, Laura has memories of her grandmother serving a bologna sandwich to her grandfather at 11:30 a.m. every day, and he would promptly thank her with a kiss on the forehead. They would finish their sandwiches over a few hands of Cribbage and would rise together to clear the table before going their separate ways.

Review the four time periods in any given day that can be the catalyst for exchanges of physical affection, affirmation, or conversation. Discuss how you can punctuate each moment with a special ritual that is the same today as it will be many years from now, and that will become the tradition of your love. Jot down your ideas here.

When we go to bed:

When we wake up:

When we leave home:

When we return home:

Conversation Questions

- When life gets especially busy and chaotic, what special ritual helps you feel grounded and secure?
- Do we have a special annual tradition as a couple? If not, what is something we can start, and when would it be?
- What is another couple's special tradition or ritual that we respect, and how can we implement this into our lives?
- What other rituals of connection would I like to implement that we haven't previously practiced?
- What is one thing each day that would help you feel loved by me (e.g., a kiss good morning or good night)?
- What kind of a ritual can we put into place that would help us stay on track with everything we are learning in this workbook?
- In what special ways can we honor our love and celebrate our commitment to each other right now?

Ritual of Connection

Before starting intimate conversations, take a moment to prepare a drink or snack that you especially enjoy. Perhaps it's a warm cup of coffee or tea, which have a ritual of preparation. As you prepare, open your senses and practice mindfulness as you complete this task. Share in the ritual together and enjoy the moment of connection.

CHAPTER 7

Envisioning Our Future

You've journeyed through the past, embraced the present, and now you're standing on the brink of the future—your shared future. This is the grand finale, the pièce de résistance, the moment when the two of you become the architects of your future.

Why is this so crucial? Envisioning your future together isn't just wishful thinking; it's the blueprint for your shared adventure. This chapter is a rendezvous of dreams, where you toss caution to the wind and let your imagination run wild. And remember, this isn't just about building a future; it's about building it *together*. By the way, nice work making it this far! Remember to *play* a bit with these exercises and conversations.

Trips We Want to Take

Maybe you've traveled a lot already. Maybe you're more inclined to stay close to home. Either way, envisioning future travels can spark excitement and reinforce the notion that your relationship is a journey. This section is like unfolding a map and marking destinations that ignite your shared wanderlust.

What destinations hold a special place in your hearts, and how can exploring these destinations strengthen your shared vision? This is less about itinerary and finances than it is about crafting a narrative of adventure. That can mean anything from backyard camping to lavish resorts. Cast your eyes to the horizon to bring an extra measure of confidence to your shared journey.

Exercise

Important conversations can be divided into three categories: dreaming, discussing, and deciding. For now, the trips you want to take fall firmly into the *dream* category. It keeps you from limiting the possibilities of play and adventure, but it's not intended to live in reality yet.

If your partner dreams of something that doesn't resonate with you, that's okay. *Dreaming* together doesn't always mean *doing* together. So consider this a "yes, and" exercise. Healthy relationships are supportive of each other's separate dreams as well as shared dreams.

A. Look at travel magazines, websites, and the map below to identify destinations that spark excitement in you. Throw all your ideas out there and create a list of 15 destinations in the spaces provided.

B. List the specific attractions or sights you wish to see at those various destinations.

C. List any experiences specific to those destinations you'd like to try.

D. List the various cuisines and traditional dishes you'd like to taste while in that region of the world.

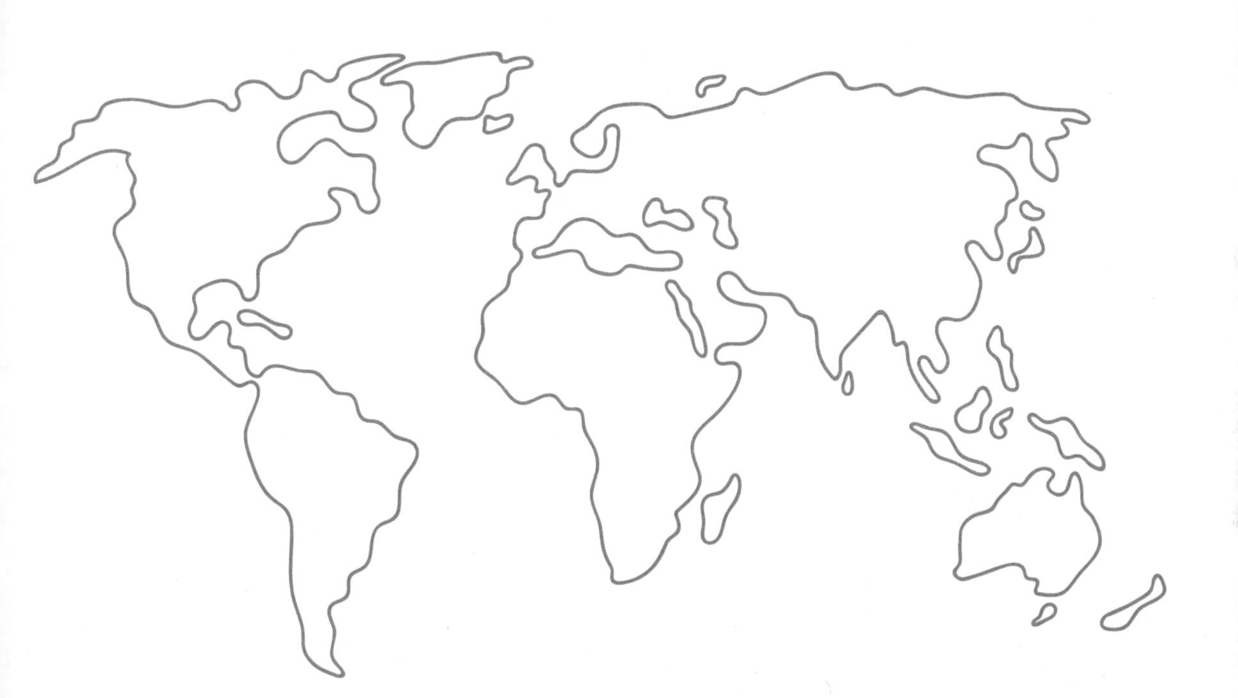

Destinations to visit:

Sights/attractions to see:

Experiences to have:

Cuisines/dishes to try:

Conversation Questions

- What is one of your favorite traveling experiences, and what made it your favorite?
- What is your preferred style of vacationing (e.g., structured itinerary, unplanned, adventurous, luxurious accommodations, relaxing)?
- If you had 30 days and unlimited funds, where in the world would you go, and what would you do there?
- When traveling, what strengths do we rely on in each other so everything goes smoothly?
- How would you feel about each of us traveling to separate destinations?
- How would you feel about me traveling with friends while you stay at home?
- How might vacationing together in a new location benefit our relationship?
- What parts of the world would we like to avoid, and why?
- What is the one destination, experience, or attraction that sparks the absolute most excitement in you, and why?

Ritual of Connection

Next time you are in line at the grocery store or find yourself at a bookstore, snag yourself a travel magazine. Flip through the pages of the travel magazine together and allow yourselves limitless dreaming of the locations you can see, activities you can experience, cuisines you can taste, and cultures you can immerse yourself in.

Dates We Want to Plan

Expand your idea of "date night" by creating a shared storyboard of how you'd like to share quality time—just you two. But first you'll need to draw on the past for inspiration. What experiences, from cozy coffee dates to complicated escape rooms, form the experiential highlights of your relationship?

Here you'll explore how to take the best of what was and update it for the future. This isn't just about where you'll go; it's about the emotions and connections you'll cultivate along the way. It's about the shared experiences that will add depth to your relationship and the necessary planning that can turn this excitement into a reality.

Exercise

SUPPLIES: mason jar or bowl, 50 strips of paper, and markers

1. Stretch outside of your comfort zone to create novel experiences in your romantic life by creating a date jar filled with doable local activities.

   Grab your search engines and look up activities within a 30-mile radius of your home. From these activities, try to identify 25 you want to experience with your partner. Write them on the strips of paper, fold them up, and put them in the jar or bowl.

2. For your date jar to be successful, establish a ritualized date night, whether it's once a week, every other week, or once a month. Once you have established when date nights will be, pull a strip of paper from the date jar and do that activity. Keep in mind that sometimes you'll need to arrange for your adventure. For example, you may need a few weeks or more if tickets have to be purchased or reservations need to be made. In the meantime, choose an activity you *can* do. When your date jar starts to get low, it's time to refill it!

Conversation Questions

* What makes you feel most connected, accepted, and loved on a date night?
* How do you feel about double dates or group dates?
* What kinds of date activities have you enjoyed most in the past?
* Do you have any sexual expectations around date nights?
* What do we think makes a date night special from any other time we are alone together?
* How do you want to feel when we are on a date?
* Do you have any limitations/restrictions around date night I should know about?
* How can we spark more fun and excitement in our relationship?
* Which date-night activities would make our hearts sing?

Ritual of Connection

Reminisce over the last fun date you had together. Agree on where and when and what took place. Take turns sharing what made it unique and special. See if you can recall all five senses: taste, touch, sound, smell, and sight. Share those sensations with each other and do your best to savor the part of their experience that is different from yours.

Our 5- to 10-Year Plan

You might think that making a 5- to 10-year plan belongs only to areas of business, finance, or career development, but why shouldn't your relationship receive the same kind of organized attention? Imagine this section as a strategic meeting for your partnership—where you align on goals, dreams, and the path to prosperity. How can your aspirations intertwine to create a vision that propels you both forward?

As you ponder your goals for security and prosperity, focus on the question of what you can achieve together that you might struggle with alone. This isn't a discussion about numbers and timelines; it's about painting the landscape of your future together.

Exercise

1. For each of the 11 life domains, rate where you *currently* are in that domain on a scale of 1 to 10 (with 1 being "needs lots of attention" and 10 being "mastered or highly satisfied").

LIFE DOMAIN	PARTNER A	PARTNER B
Physical well-being		
Mental well-being		
Environment/surroundings		
Hobbies/joy/restoration		
Romance		
Friends		
Family		

LIFE DOMAIN	PARTNER A	PARTNER B
Finances		
Purpose or work		
Spirituality		
Personal growth		

2. See where your ratings line up. For now, you'll be working together as a team. You can each do this exercise individually at another time if you'd like.

3. If you both chose 8 or above in any domain, you might not need to focus on improving that rating in your 5- to 10-year plan. Turn your attention to lower ratings. Focusing on those domains going forward can help you create more life balance and direction in your next decade.

    A. For each domain you choose to focus on, brainstorm together to create a goal statement (what you hope to achieve). Remember to DREAM BIG!

    B. Now create a why statement for each of those goals to nail down your values.

    C. Finally, lock in a handful of benchmarks or small steps along the way to your goal.

4. Here's an example of dreaming big in one of these domains:

DOMAIN: Physical well-being

Goal: We will complete all six World Marathon Majors.

"Why?" statement: We want to continue to push the limits of our mental and physical grit, feeling grateful for our bodies that continue to serve us.

Benchmarks: Join charity team that grants registrations to majors. Join running community and begin training for first marathon. lose extra 25 pounds to take pressure off joints when running. Work with a personal trainer and run coach. Allocate funds for travel to compete in one marathon a year.

DOMAIN:

Goal:

"Why?" statement:

Benchmarks:

DOMAIN:

Goal:

"Why?" statement:

Benchmarks:

DOMAIN:

Goal:

"Why?" statement:

Benchmarks:

DOMAIN:

Goal:

"Why?" statement:

Benchmarks:

DOMAIN:

Goal:

"Why?" statement:

Benchmarks:

Conversation Questions

* What do you think life is going to be like 5 to 10 years from now?
* How do you define success or personal mastery?
* How do you think our life domain priorities should shift over the next 5 to 10 years to adjust to changes?
* Which priorities and values do you want to keep throughout life, no matter what?
* Which life domain does each of us do a good job of prioritizing?
* Is there anything you're aware of that will be a major hurdle toward accomplishing one of our goals?
* Who can motivate us and propel us closer to our goals?
* What have you always wanted to do but have been too afraid to try?
* What sacrifices will we need to make to accomplish our big goals?
* Is there a relationship we need to build or connection we need to make to accomplish a goal?

Ritual of Connection

Play a quick game of Future Favorites, where each of you takes turns sharing your favorite prediction for the next 5 to 10 years. It could be a personal goal, a dream destination, or a shared aspiration. Sharing these aloud should set you up for playful and hopeful conversations about what's next for you as a couple and as individuals.

How We See Retirement

Some of Zach's most challenging clients are those who are entering the post-career phase with an empty nest. He helps them find new meaning and create a vision for something better than couples tend to do at this stage. Just as he's done with his clients, here we ask you to picture your retirement as a garden: What flowers do you want to see bloom during this vibrant stage of life? As you discuss your post-work vision, consider the values and dreams that feel important to you beyond the daily grind of work. What do you see yourself doing? What will be important to you, individually and as a couple?

This section is simply the beginning of collecting fertile seeds. It isn't a discussion of financial plans; you have your accountant for that. Rather, this is about preparing your soil for a lush, fulfilling post-work life together. Don't be afraid to dream . . . that's why you work so hard in the first place.

Exercise

1. Review the following list of plans people might make for their retirement. Do any of them resonate with your vision of retirement? Go through the list, and using different-colored pens or pencils, take turns circling any that resonate with you. It's okay to circle the same ones!

Continue to work (no retirement)

Cruise around the world

Engage in hobbies

Enjoy beach life

Garden

Go back to school

Join a sports team

Live in luxury and indulge in the finer things in life

Move into a retirement community

Play golf

Pursue an encore career

Read a lot

Reconnect with friends and family

Spend time with grandchildren (if any)

Start a business

Stay at home and just relax

Teach

Volunteer

Watch television/movies

Work part-time

Write a book

Other: ________________

Other: ________________

Other: ________________

Other: ________________

2. Look at where you align and where you differ. Talk about how you can each support the other in pursuing their dreams and where you can pursue them together to set yourselves up for a fulfilling retirement as a couple.

Conversation Questions

- How do you anticipate feeling when your work life comes to an end?
- Are you looking forward to more time once you retire or are you dreading it?
- How active would you like our social life to be when we're retired?
- What aspects of retirement might you not like?
- What aspects of retirement will you absolutely love?
- How do you think our relationship will be impacted by retirement?
- What are your ideal pursuits for retired life?
- How do we fit into each other's dream for retirement?
- In what ways might our dreams conflict and cause tension?
- How will you define yourself in retirement?

Ritual of Connection

Close your eyes and settle your mind. Imagine that you no longer have to work. Where are you? What are you wearing? What do your surroundings look like? What are you doing? How do you feel? Take turns describing the scene in your mind in as much detail as possible. Remember that everyone's dream of being "retired" is different.

Changing Bodies & Sexual Connection

It's inevitable that your bodies will change as you age. Here you'll explore ways to stay physically connected as you evolve into older versions of yourselves. This is about self-love and acceptance as much as it is about loving each other. This conversation offers a platform to explore changing desires and redefine what intimacy might mean for you in the future.

To ensure that your future is one marked by continued closeness and connection, this is an essential dialogue. How can you adapt to the changes in your bodies with grace and a shared understanding? What new expressions of intimacy can you envision that honor your evolving needs? Embrace the unknown with open hearts and a commitment to continuously cultivating a vibrant, fulfilling connection.

Exercise

In this "everything but" exercise, you'll explore ways to elicit pleasure from each other "above the belt." The goal of this exercise is to get creative and explore the numerous ways to give and experience pleasure without striving for an orgasm. You can use this as a check-in from time to time to keep on top of what your bodies respond to as the years pass.

A. Set the scene by creating a warm, comfortable environment where you and your partner can relax. Dim the lights to create a soft glow.

B. Wear minimal clothing (if any) and feel at peace in each other's company.

C. Remove distractions that might interfere with your mind-body connection or your connection with each other. (Distractions include time limitations, lack of privacy, fear of being heard, bright lights, full stomachs, alcohol, and screen use.)

D. Create mutual pleasure in each other's bodies by any means, but without direct stimulation of the genitals. Get creative!

E. Offer feedback. Communicate often about what areas of your body like to be touched, sucked, licked, flicked, stroked, or patted. If you experience a sensation that isn't pleasurable, give gentle feedback for change.

F. Continue giving and receiving pleasure for as long as you both agree upon.

Conversation Questions

- On which specific area of your body do you most enjoy being touched?
- What type of touch/stimulation do you enjoy most (e.g., gentle pressure, hard pressure, fingertips)?
- What distractions get in the way of your being able to fully enjoy yourself?
- What was it like for you to not have your genitals stimulated during the exercise?
- How might aging impact our sexual intimacy?
- How important is orgasm to you?
- Are there any tools (lubricant, vibrator, wedges) we can purchase to make sexual intimacy more enjoyable?

Ritual of Connection

For comfort and relaxation around physical intimacy with each other, it's important to clearly establish your boundaries regarding intimate touch at every stage of life. Take a moment to map out specific areas of your body that you are comfortable with your partner touching and areas that are off limits at this time. Check in from time to time, as this may change as your relationships to your bodies change.

Hopes & Fears

When you imagine the years to come, what dreams light you up? Conversely, what fears lurk in the corners, and how might they be understood and faced together? Surfacing these sentiments isn't a commitment to a particular path but an opportunity to pave the way for mutual support and resilience as you face the unknown.

This section helps you investigate the aspirations that have been quietly nurtured, the fears that have lingered in the shadows, and the surprise feelings that are waiting to be unveiled and acknowledged. Approach this conversation with curiosity, recognizing that hopes and fears are not static; they evolve with time and shared experiences.

Exercise

SUPPLIES: four scraps of paper, pens, and a jar

1. In this exercise, you'll speculate about your hopes and fears for your future together. To begin, write down one hope and one fear about your relationship or life in general on separate scraps of paper. (You don't have to choose the biggest hope or the deepest fear—just something that comes to mind.) Fold the scraps of paper, place them in a jar, and then take turns pulling them out one at a time.

2. Sit facing each other, read what's written, and close your eyes. Take a deep breath, and then talk calmly about the best-case scenario for each item. Talk gently about how these hopes and fears might come to life and how you might support each other through them. Your goal is to visualize a positive outcome in the midst of the unknown.
3. Keep the jar and feel free to put hopes and fears into it anytime. Then return to this exercise whenever you feel the need or desire to connect around your hopes and fears.

Conversation Questions

- What are some of your biggest hopes and dreams for our future together?
- What are some of your deepest fears or concerns about our future together?
- How can we help each other find strength in facing the unknown?
- How can we strike a balance between being optimistic about the future while also being realistic about potential challenges?
- How can we cultivate resilience as a couple to weather life's ups and downs?
- How would we describe our ideal future together, and what steps can we take to turn this vision into reality?
- Are there specific areas where we benefit from seeking outside guidance or support?
- How might professional help enhance our journey together?
- How can we learn to embrace uncertainty as a natural part of life's journey?
- How does embracing the unknown together strengthen our bond?
- How can we stay connected and supportive of each other during times of change and transition?

Ritual of Connection

Today is your lucky day. You just found a genie's lamp and have been granted three wishes. The only catch is that your first wish must be something only your partner can fulfill someday. Use the first two wishes for each of you individually. The third wish is for you both. Reveal your wishes to each other and commit to making them come true together.

Discussing Our Mortality

Pondering your mortality is more than just a necessary dialogue; it's an act of profound love and foresight. This conversation is important for couples of all ages, but it can be challenging. We'll help you along the way.

In this conversation you'll explore your expectations surrounding death and dying to solidify your commitment to each other as you envision your future. You may go into this conversation without being clear on what you want. Who better to figure this out with than each other? Remember, these kinds of difficult conversations can draw you closer when tackling the topic together.

Exercise

In the "this or that" game, you'll make your wishes known to your partner with regard to your preferences surrounding your death. Sure, it's a little morbid, but it's also an essential eye-opener. Take turns choosing "this" or "that" and notice how your preferences compare. Have a conversation around anything that surprises you.

THIS	THAT
Social media announcement	Obituary
Cremation	Burial
Open viewing	Closed
Organ donation	No organ donation
Grave marker	Park bench memorial
Traditional service	Celebration of life

THIS	THAT
Religious leader	Family/friend host
Meaningful eulogy	Funny eulogy
Small gathering	Large gathering
Flowers	Donation
Indoor gathering	Outdoor gathering
Framed photos	Slideshow/video
Potluck gathering	Catered event

Conversation Questions

- What are your thoughts and feelings about death?
- What does "dignity in death" mean to you?
- What do you think happens after we die?
- If I were to die first, what would you do to cope initially after losing me?
- Do you have any specific end-of-life wishes?
- Is there anyone you would want to connect with if you knew you were dying?
- What type of spiritual or religious ritual or ceremony do you want to honor your life?
- In what physical or mental capacity would you feel that life is no longer worth living?
- What would you want for me if you were to die first?
- What do you want to make sure people remember about you?

Ritual of Connection

Think back to a memorial, funeral, or celebration of life you attended together. Talk about your experience, in particular the emotions you experienced while participating in this end-of-life ritual. What was it like for you to be together during such an emotionally rich event?

Our Legacy

As you peer into the future, contemplating the legacy you leave behind goes beyond the realms of inheritances and family dynamics. This section helps you frame the lasting influence you can have on your community and the world.

This conversation isn't just about managing your resources; it's about the impact you wish to imprint on the world. In contemplating your legacy, you're not merely calculating direct impact; you're crafting a narrative of shared values and the mark you leave on the world—a mark that extends far beyond the reach of traditional family legacies and into the broader tapestry of humanity.

Exercise

In this "three pillars of legacy" exercise, you'll begin to envision how to deploy your resources in a meaningful way. The three pillars will help you to explore your ideas as a couple to better hone your vision.

Imagine the pillars as holding up the overall vision and values you have for your shared story. In each pillar, write down a few things that support that vision, using the prompts to help you brainstorm what to explore in more detail together.

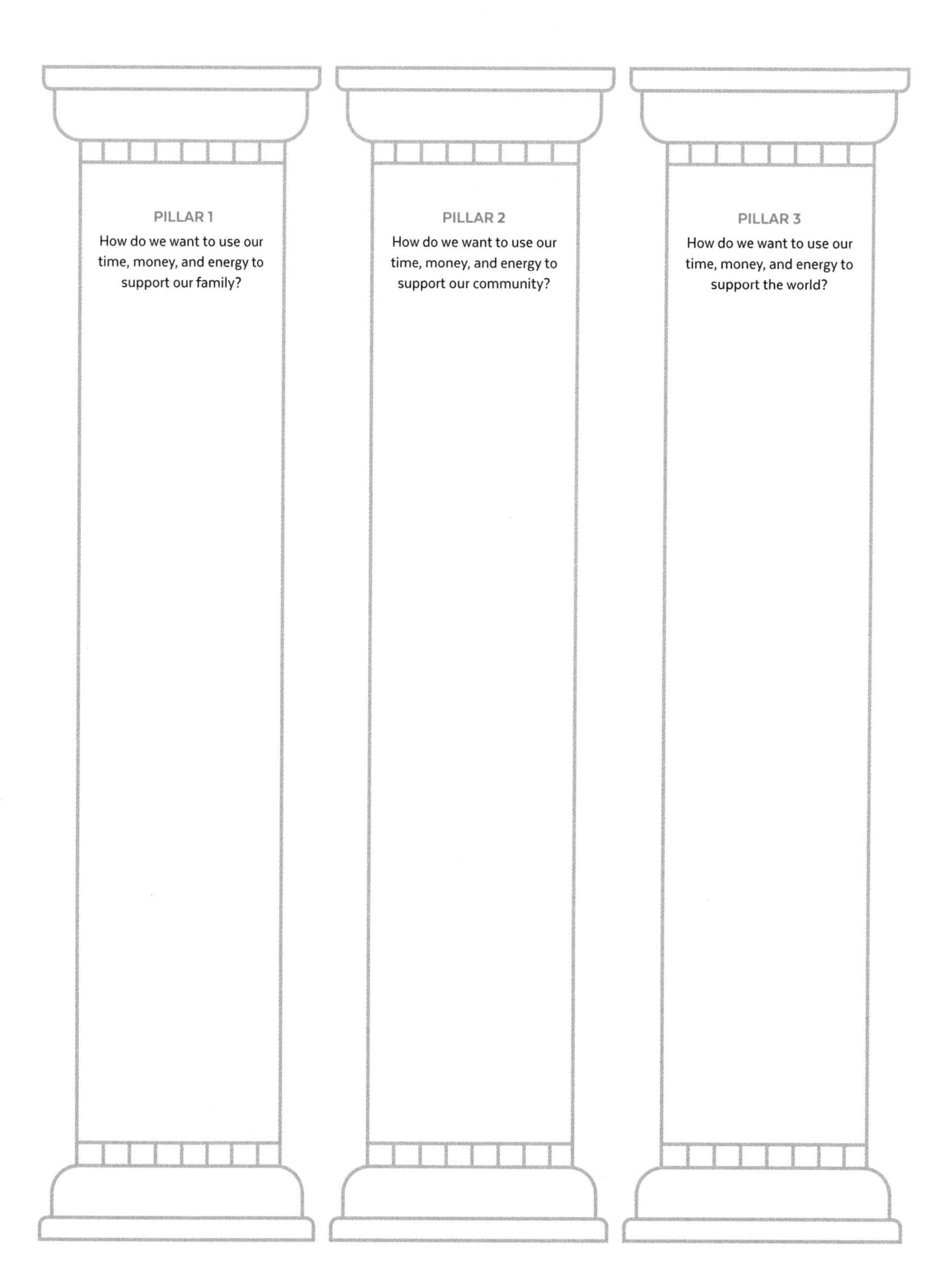
PILLAR 1
How do we want to use our time, money, and energy to support our family?
PILLAR 2
How do we want to use our time, money, and energy to support our community?
PILLAR 3
How do we want to use our time, money, and energy to support the world?

Conversation Questions

- What kind of legacy did your parents or grandparents leave behind?
- Is there someone from your past who helped influence the person you are today?
- What accomplishments do you want to be remembered for?
- Were you encouraged to give time, talent, or treasure to make the world a better place?
- What three values are most important to you?
- What kind of a financial legacy do we want to leave behind, and to whom?
- What would feel truly honoring to you that would bear your name and memory?
- In what way are you most proud to have influenced and shaped another's life?

Ritual of Connection

Imagine that the two of you were gifted $10 million to use for charitable purposes. What kind of an organization would the two of you create, and what would be the mission of this organization? What kind of an impact do you think $10 million could make?

The Story of Us

Years from now, when people recount the tale of your love, resilience, and dreams, what story do you want them to tell? This is an opportunity to give voice to the anecdotes that will make people smile—the tales that will inspire them in their own relationships.

As you explore this topic, consider the milestones as well as the small moments that define your unique narrative. Pull back the veil on your adventures, inside jokes, and shared values. Enjoy the opportunity to paint a vivid, delightful narrative that will be a testament to enduring love and shared joy.

Exercise

SUPPLIES: four index cards or similar-size paper

1. Write "ME" on two of the cards and "YOU" on the other two. Each partner gets one of each.
2. Face each other and hold your cards close to you without revealing the words.
3. Take turns reading the questions. When the reader says, "Go," both partners show the card that reveals their answer.
4. Spend a moment or two discussing any differences, and then move on. You can always revisit the conversation later.

QUESTIONS

Who was more interested in the other when we first started dating?

Who fell in love with the other first?

Who is more likely to apologize first?

Who is more emotionally intelligent?

Who is better with money?

Who is most likely to put their own needs before anyone else's?

Who is better liked by our in-laws?

Who is most likely to avoid a conflict?

Who is most likely to discuss our private life in public?

Who is most likely to want to touch toes in bed?

Who is most likely to initiate a new sex position?

Who is most likely to request watching a movie or reading a book together?

Who is most likely to surprise the other person with a gift?

Who is most likely to be grumpy when we are hungry?

Conversation Questions

- Which of our dating stories would others find amusing or romantic?
- What tender, vulnerable moment that we shared along the way would make a good scene in a movie?
- What details of when we first moved in together stand out as particularly memorable?
- If our relationship was a TV series, what era represents the highest drama?
- What was it like meeting each other's parents for the first time?
- Thinking of our relationship as a quest, what are some of our most meaningful "side journeys"?
- If we were to renew our vows, what would differ from how we did our wedding?
- Knowing what we know now, would we tell stories of our shared journey any differently than we used to?
- In the coming years, what stories do we want to share with others about our life together?

Ritual of Connection

If only one photo of you as a couple survived long after you were gone, which photo would you want it to be? Go through your photos, including any old photo albums or stacks of printed photos, and select your favorite couple photo, one that embodies your love for each other. Frame it and put it somewhere you will see it often.

Closing the Conversation: A Journey beyond Words

Congratulations on working—or talking—your way through these meaningful conversations! You've gone deeper than most couples manage to, delving into the depths of shared experiences, dreams, and vulnerabilities. As you reach the final pages of this conversational odyssey, take a moment to appreciate the distance you've covered and the connections you've strengthened.

Remember, this workbook is just a guide. You're not finished with your efforts to reconnect. You're just getting started with a journey that will continue beyond these pages. Take a moment to celebrate the progress you've made and acknowledge the courage it took to engage in these conversations. This is a testament to your commitment to each other and the resilience of your love.

To keep the momentum alive, practice the art of intentional listening—truly hearing each other with an open heart. Continue scheduling regular check-ins, creating a dedicated time and space for connection amid life's hustle. Embrace novelty; introduce new topics and experiences into your dialogue, ensuring your conversations evolve with the changing seasons of your lives. Most importantly, extend the same grace and compassion to yourselves that you've generously given each other throughout this process.

A lifetime of conversation and connection awaits you. Check out the appendix to help you pick up right where this workbook leaves off. And be sure to revisit this workbook whenever you need a nudge. For now we'll raise a glass and say, "Cheers! Here's to a lifetime of continued discovery, laughter, and profound connection."

Appendix: Navigating Future Conversations

As you step out of the structured pages of this workbook, let the following templates serve as your conversation compass, ready to guide you through the uncharted territories of invigorating and challenging conversations alike. Crafted with care, these templates are bonus tools, an added layer of support for the ever-evolving dialogue that will shape your relationship.

We're confident that your conversations can remain intentional, heartfelt, and uniquely yours as long as you remain committed to curiosity and compassion. Take comfort in knowing that you've already built the essential skills you need to enjoy the relationship you desire and deserve.

Healthy Dialogue Template

A healthy dialogue between two people assumes an exchange of ideas, full of curiosity, openness, and respect. This template reminds you of key communication components for healthy dialogue.

1. **Check in with yourselves.** Are you each entering this conversation as your best self? Do you feel safe, calm, and connected? If so, you are ready to chat. (See page 50 for a checklist.)
2. **Get clear on the purpose of your dialogue.** Are you here to dream, discuss, or decide? (See page 12.)
3. **Get clear on your roles.** What kind of a listener does the speaker need right now? Do you need your listener to play devil's advocate, offer advice, empathize, point out your blind spots, just listen, or something else?
4. **Repair, repair, repair!** With emotionally charged topics, it isn't a matter of *if* your conversation gets off track, it's a matter of *when*

it gets off track. Remember, simple phrases like "Hey, I think I blew that. Can I try that again?" or "I want to make this better, but I don't know how" can keep your conversation from devolving.

5. **Know when it's time to stop.** We all know what it feels like when communication stops being productive and moves into a hurtful place. Make an agreement to pause the conversation and take at least a 20-minute break. (See "Understand Your Limits" on page 31.)

Guidelines for the Speaker

* Soften your communication by speaking about your own needs, fears, and hopes by using "I statements" (e.g., "I feel overwhelmed about XYZ and would appreciate if you would help by doing XYZ").
* Avoid inflammatory language, which tends to unnecessarily intensify communication. Throw out words like "always," "never," and "should" as well as curse words.
* Be willing to be open and vulnerable. Communicating your feelings opens the door to intimacy.

Guidelines for the Listener

* Stay attuned to the speaker by listening not only to the words but also to tone of voice, body language, and what is *not* being said.
* Practice active listening. Make sure the speaker knows that you understand what they are saying by repeating it back (e.g., "I think what you are saying is X, Y, Z. Do I have it right?").
* Validate the speaker. Recognize and accept the speaker's feelings (e.g., "Of course you are overwhelmed by that situation; you have so little time and so much to do").

How to Open a Casual or Lighthearted Topic

Initiating a lighthearted conversation is sort of like perusing the menu at your favorite restaurant—it's casual, fun, and sets a breezy tone. Consider lighthearted conversation as anything that brings smiles to your faces—from sharing childhood antics to dreaming about your future travel destinations.

1. Decide in advance to give your partner the benefit of your goodwill toward them.
2. Lead with smiles, laughter, and *playful* teasing.
3. Open the conversation with a topic like, "What would it be like if our neighbor's dog had superpowers and we were the only ones who knew?" or "If we had a magic portal, where would we agree to go right now?"

This workbook had many conversation questions that likely kept you both feeling relaxed and lighthearted. However, you probably also experienced that intense emotions can show up quickly and turn up the heat fast, so tread carefully.

Back off if one or both of you gets dysregulated. Pause and acknowledge the shift. Express understanding and ask whether the other wants to continue or take a break. If it becomes too emotionally charged, a well-timed pause for at least 20 minutes would be a wise move. Most of all, be patient; conversation is both a skill and an art. Mastery takes time.

How to Open Emotionally Charged Topics

Opening an emotionally charged conversation is like hiking into darkening woods—it requires finesse and care. What qualifies as charged will vary, but if the emotional stakes feel high, you're in the territory. It could be anything from past wounds to future fears. Remember, some topics will always spark heat, and that's part of every relationship.

Challenging conversations might include past arguments/how you handle conflict as a couple, the impact of each other's families on your life and how that shapes your relationship, individual needs in intimacy, and financial goals.

1. When facing charged topics, first be sure there are no distractions.
2. Approach with a soft start-up. It's always a good idea to ask, "Is now a good time?"
3. Use eye contact or a gentle touch.
4. If met with reluctance, show patience and create a safe space. You may need to signal the importance of the topic with a calm but assertive tone.
5. Open with something like "I've sensed tension around XYZ. Can we share our perspectives and find common ground?"
6. Lead by using "I statements." Express your feelings and give your partner the opportunity to do the same.
7. If one or both of you becomes dysregulated (see page 31 for the signs to be on the lookout for), acknowledge the emotional shift. Check in with each other and decide whether you should continue or take a break. Remember that charged topics may need multiple conversations.

Resources

Come as You Are: The Surprising New Science That Will Transform Your Sex Life **by Emily Nagoski, PhD (Simon & Schuster Paperbacks, 2015, 2021)**

Emily Nagoski's book demystifies the science of sex so that everyone can create a better sex life and discover more pleasure than they ever thought possible.

Eight Dates: Essential Conversations for a Lifetime of Love **by John Gottman, PhD, Julie Schwartz Gottman, PhD, Doug Abrams, and Rachel Carlton Abrams, MD (Workman Publishing Co., 2018)**

The Gottmans' research is the gold standard for science-based relationship principles. This book takes your conversations into actual dates, inviting you to apply your skills in the real world.

The 80/80 Marriage: A New Model for a Happier, Stronger Relationship **by Nate Klemp, PhD, and Kaley Klemp (Penguin Life, 2021)**

Nate and Kaley Klemp propose the notion of "radical generosity" in this excellent book on shared responsibility in marriage.

The New Rules of Marriage: What You Need to Know to Make Love Work **by Terrence Real (Ballantine Books, 2007)**

Terrence Real's book invites couples into an empowered relationship by encouraging both partners to explore one key question: "How do I give you what you need in order for me to get what I want?"

We've Had This Fight Before: A Brief Guide on Why Couples Fight and What to Do about It **by Claudia Grauf-Grounds, PhD (Honors Press, 2017)**

This is one of our favorite books for helping couples bring new skills to bear in conflict. It's an impeccably researched and eminently accessible read.

Acknowledgments

Laura: I want to thank my husband, who has always believed in me more than I believe in myself. Thank you for throwing every resource at me to accomplish my dreams and fulfill my purpose. Thank you to Zach, who has challenged my thinking and served as a sounding board this past decade. You make a great friend and mentor. Thank you to the hundreds of couples who have welcomed me into their vulnerable, scary places and taught me what true partnership looks like.

Zach: I feel immensely grateful that I am in meaningful conversation with friends, family, and clients on a regular basis. I'm thankful that I get to talk to Laura every week. Our conversations make me both smarter and wiser, and they're never boring. Thank you to our mutual friend, who is the best conversationalist I know. Thanks to Sarah—our conversations always point me in the right direction. And, finally, Rebecca, who always puts wind at my back. I'm glad and grateful that I get to stay in conversation with you daily.

About the Authors

ZACH BRITTLE, LMHC, is a licensed mental health counselor, Certified Gottman Therapist (CGT), and certified Relational Life Therapist (RLT). He is also the author of *The Relationship Alphabet* and *Marriage Therapy Journal*. Zach lives in Seattle, Washington, with his wife and two adulting daughters.

LAURA HECK, LMFT, is a licensed marriage and family therapist, certified Gottman therapist, and sex therapist in private practice, working exclusively with couples to manage conflict and deepen intimacy and pleasure. Laura has been married to her lover and best friend for the past 15 years, and they have a precocious nine-year-old son, two dogs, and a Sprinter van.

Zach and Laura are cohosts of the podcast *Marriage Therapy Radio*, where, with wit and wisdom, they tackle the most common complaints every relationship experiences.

Hi there,

We hope you found *Reconnect: A Marriage Counseling Workbook* helpful. If you have any questions or concerns about your book, or have received a damaged copy, please contact customerservice@penguinrandomhouse.com. We're here and happy to help.

Also, please consider writing a review on your favorite retailer's website to let others know what you thought of the book!

Sincerely,
The Zeitgeist Team